Shortcuts to Success

Othello

EXAM GUIDE FOR LEAVING CERTIFICATE

Anne Gormley

Gill & Macmillan

Gill & Macmillan
Hume Avenue
Park West
Dublin 12
with associated companies throughout the world
www.gillmacmillan.ie

© Anne Gormley 2014
978 07171 4868 4

Print origination in Ireland by O'K Graphic Design, Dublin

The paper used in this book is made from the wood pulp of managed forests.
For every tree felled, at least one tree is planted, thereby renewing natural resources.

Any links to external websites should not be construed as an endorsement by Gill & Macmillan of the content or view of the linked material. Furthermore it cannot be guaranteed that all external links will be live.

CONTENTS

Acknowledgements

I wish to thank the late Eilish O'Brien for allowing me to use her notes and for all her help and support.

BACKGROUND NOTES ON THE PLAY *OTHELLO*

The play was written in 1603. Shakespeare's comedy *Measure for Measure* (1604) has certain similarities with *Othello*. In both plays the theme of temptation is a crucial aspect. Both plays are based on Shakespeare's reading of Giraldi Cinthio's *Hecatommithi* (1564).

Shakespeare did not rely on one source only while writing Othello. The play was also shaped by other readings of Shakespeare at this time, among them *The Geographical History of Africa* published in 1600 and a book on the Constitution of Venice written by Lewes Lewkenor. *Pliny's History of the World* translated into English by Philemon Holland was another source for the play.

Much of the magnificent imagery that Shakespeare uses in this play comes from Philemon Holland's vivid prose: the exotic medicinal gum from the Arabian tree and images such as 'not poppy, not mandragora, nor all the drowsy syrups of the world'.

Part of the background of this play arises from the clash between Christian and Muslim cultures. The play is set in Venice, which could be seen as a meeting place between east and west. There was a fascination with the exotic 'other' among the groundlings and the court of Elizabeth I. Shakespeare knew that a play about racism towards black people would be of interest to a London audience of the time, since London was home to several thousand black people who were employed mainly as servants, dancers and entertainers.

There were mixed reactions to the various performances of the play. It was dramatised at court and in the different provinces. Some critics saw it as a warning to maidens not to run away with Blackamoors. John Adams, a U.S. president in the early nineteenth century, reacted to the play by saying that 'black and white blood cannot be intermingled in marriage without a gross outrage upon the laws of Nature'. The play continued to cause controversy right into the twentieth century: some audiences in Britain in the 1950s were quite shocked by the play's overt displays of emotion and the fact that the actors kissed on the stage.

The play certainly emerges as a powerful representation of human nature and as one of Shakespeare's supreme masterpieces. In this play, he has managed to construct a powerful vision of how pure evil can operate to undermine truth and goodness and to deceive a human person to such an extent that they are incapable of distinguishing between what is real and what is false. The play continues to offer many valuable insights on history and on politics today.

THE NOTION OF SHAKESPEAREAN TRAGEDY

The two traditional forms of drama are comedy and tragedy. Comedy laughs at humanity's disruptive instincts and passions. Tragedy, on the other hand, analyses the motivations behind people's actions, in particular those that disrupt the social order. The results of this disruption lead to the death of the main protagonist. In tragedy, the action always ends in the death of the leading character.

Shakespeare wrote four main tragedies: *Macbeth*, *King Lear*, *Hamlet* and *Othello*.

There is also a strong focus on the roots of evil in humankind. This evil is rooted in the freedom of the person and results in death – the deaths not only of the bad characters, but also of those who are innocent.

All great tragedies force us to ask some very difficult questions:

- Can virtue and good qualities survive in a world that seems to be dominated by evil and destruction?
- What place does freedom have in the whole question of evildoing?
- How much does the will of the person influence their behaviour, particularly in the case of wrongdoing?

In this play, we witness how Othello, a Moor who is living in Venice, becomes the victim of tragic circumstances on account of certain flaws in his nature. The play dramatises how the tragic hero is deluded in his judgement about people and the tragic consequences that emerge as a result. It also shows the powerful operations of evildoing and how goodness can be used to facilitate evil.

There is a basic **pattern** in a tragedy.

- The tragic hero is generally a person who plays a prominent role in the social order, such as a king, a general or a great soldier.
- This person has a huge capacity for achieving heroic action and moral greatness.
- Through his use of freedom and conscience, his life is thrown into confusion and discord.
- This experience of confusion and discord extends to all of his relationships and all aspects of his life.
- The sense of strife and dissension is generally of an **extreme** nature.

- Life becomes chaotic and meaningless for the main protagonist.
- The tragic hero reaches a state of **recognition** about the implications of his flaw – on himself and his life in general.
- The culmination of the action lies in the death of the tragic hero.
- Good triumphs at the conclusion and the forces of evil are vanquished, but not without causing a great deal of harm.

So there is a certain movement in tragedy. The tragic hero moves from a state of high status professionally, socially, morally and psychologically. The movement of the main character or protagonist is downward, through **suffering**. Part of the tragic process involves perception within the tragic hero of the implications of his flaw on his own life and on the lives of the people around him. This perception or **insight** on the part of the tragic hero is important, since it enables the audience to retain sympathy with him through his state of destitution and loss.

Tragedy also deals with **realistic events** and **realistic people**. The audience must be able to identify with and understand the emotions reflected in a tragedy. Usually, the tragic hero's flaw involves a misjudgement or an error of some type, and this is made by a person **with *full freedom***, aware of what they are doing and aware of the consequences of their actions.

It is essential that the dramatist can gain the sympathy of the audience for the tragic hero. This presupposes that an audience can identify with the hero and recognise in him a similar humanity and capacity for both greatness and error. The tragic hero must be a person who can stand for us and reflect all aspects of our human nature.

THE SOLILOQUY IN SHAKESPEARE'S TRAGEDIES

The soliloquy in drama is a speech by a character, which is addressed to the audience. Drama is an ideal form for the soliloquy, since an actor can face an audience directly from the stage and convey certain emotions by means of facial and bodily gestures. The soliloquy in Shakespeare would have been addressed to an Elizabethan audience from a stage that protruded into the pit, and the audience would have been sitting, or standing in some cases, on three sides. This afforded Shakespeare an excellent means of developing the plot of his dramas. The soliloquy allows an audience to enter into the mind of a character and to begin to understand the various emotions and conflicts within that person. It gives the audience an insight into the soul and inner workings of a character's mindset that is more difficult to gain from dialogue.

Through the language and imagery used in a soliloquy, an audience can see, hear and feel all that a character is expressing. The soliloquy becomes a very powerful means of showing character and motivation, and the development of the plot.

THE ASIDE IN SHAKESPEARE'S TRAGEDIES

Like the soliloquy, an aside is a short speech that is expressed by a character directly to the audience. It differs in length from the soliloquy, but in general it has the same function, which is to give the audience an insight into the soul and motivations of a character.

See also the Summary of Soliloquies and Asides (p.71).

OTHELLO AS A TRAGEDY

Othello is one of Shakespeare's four great tragedies, the other three being *Hamlet, King Lear* and *Macbeth*. Of the four plays, *Othello* is the one that sticks closest to the classical norms of tragedy. It is a tightly-plotted story about an exceptionally great man who is partially brought down because of a defect in his character and a defective vision of the world around him.

Othello is an excellent commander – brave, intelligent and efficient. What is it then that allows him to be brought so low by the mean-spirited Iago?

The answer must lie in the fact that Othello is very **self-conscious about being different** from the Venetians. He is aware of the connotations they have invented and associated with his skin colour. To them, black men are sexual predators and barbarians, men who indulge in witchcraft and other unchristian practices. In effect, Othello's impeccable manners and refined speech may seem to be an exaggerated attempt on his part to be accepted by the people of his adopted city. This is a sign of his **insecurity**. Othello needs to be sure that he is accepted. Desdemona's love is his palpable proof that he is so. When he meets her at the port in Cyprus, he declares that she is his **'soul's joy'**, adding that she is the calm that follows the storm. This metaphor is important. Desdemona represents for him the calm. He is dependent on her not only as a normal source of love, but as a guarantee of order, and of life making sense for him. In addition she represents a calm that makes the storm worthwhile in his life. *'When I love thee not'*, he tells her, *'chaos is come again.'* A return to chaos is for him intolerable. Iago perceives this, and therefore he knows precisely how he will destroy this man he passionately hates.

Why does Iago *'hate the Moor'* so passionately? What is his motive? He mentions various reasons – the fact that Othello made Cassio his lieutenant rather than himself. He also believes that Othello has slept with his wife Emilia. But we may well conclude with Coleridge that Iago is simply **a man of hate** and that his citing of different reasons for wishing to destroy Othello is nothing more than *'the motive-hunting of a motiveless malignancy'. He* has no true motive. He wants to destroy the Moor simply because he hates him. Iago is an evil man and needs no other motive.

In his book *Poetics*, Aristotle maintained that tragic drama is an imitation of life. For Aristotle, tragedy is 'an imitation of an action which is serious and complete, and which has a kind of magnitude...it is dramatic and not narrative in form. Through pity and fear it accomplishes a purgation of the emotions.'

Shakespeare manages to do this in his play *Othello*. The play shows us the **tragic consequences of deception and misjudgement** of people and situations. We are offered, through tragic catharsis, a view of human motivation in some very complex situations, and also the experience of death.

The chilling consequences of moral evil are fatal in all of Shakespeare's tragedies. In *Othello*, the **power of love and loyalty** are also evident. Humans are faced with the consequences of surviving the mess caused by evildoing, and the duty to keep going in the interests of the state and of society in general.

The error or flaw in Othello is basically **blindness to human nature** and in particular to the nature of his ensign Iago. Othello trusts totally in the 'honesty' of Iago and this mistaken trust becomes the means through which Iago's devious and diabolic plot flourishes so well.

Othello freely allows himself to be tempted by Iago into believing that his wife has betrayed him by sleeping with Cassio, a Lieutenant in the Venetian army. Through a series of subtle insinuations and deliberate temptations in Act III, scene iii, Othello allows himself to become so consumed with anger and jealousy that he resolves to murder his wife Desdemona. This tragic action caused by blindness and rash judgement results in catastrophe – the death of Desdemona, and soon after that of Emilia at the hands of her husband.

It is only at the conclusion of this tragic play that Othello actually sees Iago for what he truly is: a devious **manipulator**. We are left at the end of the play with the chilling idea that Iago's operations in the plot of the play are similar to that of a devil. Othello's passionate words to Iago are evidence of this: 'I look down towards his feet, but that's a fable,/If thou be'st a devil, I cannot kill thee.'

Evil is represented in the play by the figure of Iago. In *Othello*, a good man is ruined by a fatal flaw: blindness to human nature and its true reality. This, combined with his supreme trust in a treacherous man, causes calamity and death for both himself and those around him.

THE PLOT OF *OTHELLO*

Some critics maintain that the plot of this play is the character of Iago in action. The actual plot depends on a number of things, particularly the ready acquiescence of Othello to believe all that his wicked ensign Iago tells him. It also depends on certain other factors: the existence of Cassio, the capable and good-looking lieutenant; the innocence and virtue of Desdemona; and the fact that Roderigo allows himself to be duped by Iago. Chance and coincidence play a big part in generating the plot.

Iago stands at the centre of the plot of this play. From the outset, his hatred and inordinate jealousy provide continuous fuel to bring about the downfall of other characters. He can easily tempt Othello, a military general whose experience of life is limited to the battlefield only and who knows very little about the way human beings operate and interact. The fact that Othello is a Moor, and therefore an outsider in Venetian society, facilitates Iago's plot to a large extent. Othello allows himself to believe Iago's statements that Othello's wife has been unfaithful and has committed adultery with Cassio.

Jealousy consumes Othello and his inexperience of this emotion contributes to his tragic downfall. His rational faculty becomes clouded with passion and renders him incapable of distinguishing the truth from the lies that Iago has spun.

The accidental loss of the handkerchief, together with the thoughtless and flighty actions of Emilia in handing it to her husband, facilitates Iago's plot greatly. Iago plants this handkerchief in Cassio's apartment and later on, while tempting Othello in the garden, he uses it as evidence to frame Cassio.

On the basis of some very flimsy evidence, Othello decides to kill his wife. At the same time, he charges Iago with the commission of killing Cassio.

Iago operates like a puppeteer in the play, using all the characters as pawns to further his devious manoeuvrings. He uses the rich and foolish young man Roderigo for his money, and then manages to deceive him into believing that he will help him win the hand of Desdemona.

In the end, Iago is exposed by his wife, Emilia. Formerly, she had functioned as a superficial 'bawd' who unwittingly facilitated his wicked ploys. When the full realisation of what has happened to Desdemona is revealed in the concluding scene, Emilia has no hesitation whatever in giving her life in the service of truth. She dies at the hands of her husband, vindicating the honour and virtue of Desdemona in a truly heroic and self-sacrificing manner.

Othello is filled with remorse at what he has done and he kills himself at the end with his own sword. Iago is captured and is punished for his deeds. Cassio is appointed Lieutenant in Venice.

SUMMARY/ANALYSIS OF SCENES

ACT I SCENE I

- Iago and Roderigo are speaking disparagingly about Othello.
- Othello has promoted Cassio as a general in the Venetian army, over Iago.
- Iago intends to avenge himself on Othello.
- Iago and Roderigo rouse Brabantio, Desdemona's father, and inform him that his daughter has eloped with Othello the Moor.
- Roderigo has hopes of winning Desdemona's hand in marriage.

This scene takes place at night on a street in Venice. The themes of evil and dissimulation are introduced from the outset. Iago states that he hates Othello and is using him for his own interests.

QUESTIONS

1. What do we learn about Othello in this scene?
2. From this scene, find three quotations that sum up the character of Iago.
3. What do you learn about the plot from this scene?

ACT I SCENE II

- Iago is speaking to Othello about Brabantio's anger.
- Othello explains to Iago that he loves the gentle Desdemona.
- Cassio enters and informs Othello that he is summoned to the senate on account of a political threat from Cyprus.
- Brabantio accuses Othello of using witchcraft to seduce his daughter.

Iago's equivocal nature is shown here in his relationships with Othello. Our first impressions of Othello show us that he is a man of peace and self-control. Othello does not deny his marriage to Desdemona.

QUESTIONS

1. Contrast Iago with Othello in this scene.
2. From this scene, identify three features of Othello's character.
3. What do we learn about Brabantio in this scene?

ACT I SCENE III

- We learn from the Duke of Venice that the Turks are invading the Venetian stronghold in Cyprus.
- The Duke and senate require Othello to defend Cyprus against the impending attack from the Turks.
- Brabantio accuses Othello of bewitching his daughter with spells.
- Othello explains to the Venetian senate how he won the love of Desdemona in an honourable way.
- Desdemona confirms her love for Othello and asks that she accompany him immediately to Cyprus.
- Iago reassures Roderigo that the marriage will end.

This is another night scene. Othello's honesty and nobility are vindicated in his defence of his relationship with Desdemona before the Venetian senate. Desdemona's love for Othello is real and authentic. Iago engages in his first soliloquy, where he announces his plot to use Cassio as a pawn in order to destroy the marriage of Othello and Desdemona.

QUESTIONS

1. Othello's military prowess is evident from this scene. Identify three quotes that highlight this aspect of Othello's character.
2. What insight do you get from Desdemona's first entrance in the play?
3. Find three examples of irony in this scene and explain why they are ironic in the context of the tragedy.

ACT II SCENE I

- Montano, the governor of Cyprus, is learning about the nature of the storm at sea and how it is that Cassio has arrived before Othello.
- Desdemona and Cassio engage in some light-hearted banter.
- Othello arrives and is overwhelmed with joy to be accompanied by Desdemona.
- Iago tells Roderigo about his plans to use Cassio to undermine the marriage of Othello.

The storm at sea becomes a symbol of the massive chaos and damage that Iago will unleash with his villainous plans. Iago's control over events is revealed in the fact that the scene concludes with another soliloquy, where he speaks about arousing a damaging jealousy within Othello. The use of dramatic and situational irony are particularly important in this scene.

QUESTIONS

1. Find examples of contrasting images in this scene and comment on their function.
2. What do we learn about Iago's attitude towards Roderigo, Cassio and Desdemona from his soliloquy?
3. What new insight do we get about Cassio in this scene?

ACT II SCENES II and III

*   A proclamation is announced that celebrations will commence on two accounts: the marriage of Othello and Desdemona and the cessation of the Turkish threat on Cyprus.
*   Iago manages to get Cassio drunk. In doing so, he tarnishes Cassio's reputation in the eyes of Montano.
*   Iago provokes a fight between Roderigo and Cassio.
*   Othello loses his temper with Cassio and dismisses him from his post as general.
*   Iago advises Cassio to plead with Desdemona for reinstatement in his position.
*   Iago's 'honesty' is consolidated in the minds of the main characters because of his behaviour at the feast.
*   Iago announces his plot: he will get his wife to work for Desdemona and lead Othello to see Cassio and Desdemona talking together.

There are two other night scenes in which the evil and villainy of Iago begins to grow. Iago's capacity to manipulate people is dramatised throughout these scenes. Othello loses his temper for the first time. We gain a deeper insight into Cassio's character, his concern for 'reputation' and his gullibility and naivety in trusting Iago.

QUESTIONS

1. What new insights do we gain about the character of Desdemona in these scenes?
2. Identify the different roles that Iago adopts in these scenes.
3. Select three images used in these scenes and comment on what they reveal about the different themes in the play.

ACT III SCENE I

*   Cassio's attempts to employ musicians to entertain Othello are rebuffed.
*   Iago tells Cassio that he will furnish him with the opportunity to meet Desdemona in order to plead for his reinstatement.

Cassio's action in getting musicians to play for Othello on the morning after the feast shows him to be impulsive. It is clear that Iago's plot is developing without any obstacle.

QUESTIONS

1. Find some examples of comedy in this scene.
2. Identify irony in this scene.
3. How is Iago's plot developing in this scene?

ACT III SCENES II and III

* Othello tells Iago he will be engaged in checking the citadel and the fortifications.
* In a garden nearby, Desdemona assures Cassio that she will do her utmost to plead with Othello so that Cassio is reinstated.
* Othello and Iago join Desdemona, who immediately begins to plead for Cassio.
* When Desdemona leaves the garden, Iago suggests to Othello that something is going on between Desdemona and Cassio.
* Iago proceeds to plant doubts about Desdemona's fidelity, hinting that Venetian women betray their husbands readily.
* Othello asks Iago to find out more and to ask Emilia to watch the relationship between the two more closely.
* When Iago leaves, Othello is plagued with self-doubt and doubts about his wife.
* Desdemona arrives on the scene and realises that her husband is upset.
* In trying to help Othello, Desdemona drops her handkerchief. Emilia picks it up and gives it to her husband Iago.
* Iago decides to leave Desdemona's handkerchief in Cassio's lodging that night.
* When Othello returns, he is tortured with doubt. Iago proceeds to tell him a false story about Cassio's mutterings while he was asleep.
* Iago also tells Othello that he saw Cassio with Desdemona's handkerchief.
* Othello believes all that Iago tells him and prays that vengeance will be carried out by killing Desdemona and Cassio.

Act III, scene iii is the longest scene in the play and is usually called the 'temptation scene'. Iago exercises supreme control from the beginning to the end of this scene. We also witness the profound deterioration of Othello's character in this scene. Desdemona becomes an unwitting victim of her own essential goodness here. Emilia's thoughtless action in handing the handkerchief to her husband helps Iago's plot.

ACT III SCENE IV

- Desdemona enquires about the location of Cassio from 'a clown'.
- Othello enters and asks Desdemona for the handkerchief.
- Desdemona ignores her husband's request and insists on speaking about Cassio's reinstatement.
- Othello becomes very angry and leaves.
- Emilia and Desdemona speak about jealousy.
- Iago enters with Cassio and they speak to Desdemona and Emilia about the change in Othello.
- Bianca, a courtesan, speaks alone to Cassio about his neglect of her. He hands her the handkerchief he has found in his chamber and asks her to copy it.

This scene dramatises the role of the female characters in the play. Desdemona becomes an unwitting victim of her own goodness. Emilia is a realist and is quite cynical about love and relationships: she says that men 'are all but stomachs, and we all but food'. Bianca is a high-class prostitute who has been with Cassio for a while and feels jealous about the fact that he has been neglecting her for someone else.

ACT IV SCENE I

- Iago proceeds to plant a series of insinuations about Desdemona's infidelity with Cassio.
- Othello becomes enraged over Iago's statements and collapses on the ground.
- Cassio enters and Iago explains that Othello is experiencing epileptic fits.

- Cassio leaves. When Othello recovers, Iago explains that he will challenge Cassio to speak the truth while Othello remains hidden.
- Cassio enters and Iago speaks to him about his relationship with Bianca.
- Othello, who remains hidden, can see the scene but is unable to hear it. He misinterprets the situation and is led to believe that Cassio is speaking about Desdemona instead of Bianca.
- When Cassio leaves, Othello's anger is at a peak and he decides to kill his wife.
- Iago declares that he will kill Cassio himself.
- A letter arrives through Lodovico, Desdemona's cousin, requesting that Othello return to Venice and that Cassio take his place.
- Desdemona reacts with joy. Othello misinterprets her reaction and strikes her publicly.
- Lodovico is shocked at the dramatic change in the 'noble Moor'.
- Iago's diabolic manoeuvring reaches a climax here when he manages to convince Othello to murder his own wife. Luck and coincidence play into the hands of Iago and facilitate his plot to a great extent in this scene. Desdemona becomes an unwitting victim of her own kindness and goodness.

QUESTIONS

1. Analyse the different stages of Iago's foul plot in this scene.
2. Find three examples of irony in this scene and comment on their function in terms of character and theme.
3. According to Lodovico, what are the changes in Othello's character?

ACT IV SCENE II

- Othello proceeds to question Emilia about his wife's activities.
- Othello challenges his wife about her fidelity and accuses her of being as 'false as hell'.
- Othello treats his wife and Emilia as if they were prostitutes.
- Emilia tells her husband Iago that Othello has been deceived by some 'base notorious knave' that should be whipped.
- Roderigo is impatient, since he has given all his jewels to Iago with no prospect of getting the hand of Desdemona.
- Iago convinces Roderigo to murder Cassio and that the way will be clear for him then.

Othello's character has begun to deteriorate and this is reflected in his language patterns and use of certain images. Emilia's moral nature begins to emerge and she shows some exceptional courage in vindicating the honour of Desdemona. Roderigo is an exceptionally weak character who allows himself to be used as a pawn in the hands of Iago the villain.

> **QUESTIONS**
>
> 1. Find three images that highlight the change in Othello's character.
> 2. This scene is remarkable for its effective use of dramatic irony. Show where and how this is used.
> 3. What arguments does Iago use to manipulate Roderigo in this scene?

ACT IV SCENE III

- Desdemona speaks to Emilia about death and requests that she would be laid out in a sheet if she should die.
- Desdemona tells Emilia about a song that she learned from her maid.
- Both Emilia and Desdemona speak about infidelity.
- Desdemona declares that she would not do such a wrong 'for the whole world'.
- Emilia speaks about the fact that infidelity is a fact of life and the problem lies in the husbands' fault of not fulfilling their duties in marriage.

This is a night scene which is rich in symbolism. The scene precedes the final scene where Desdemona meets her death at the hands of Othello. The 'willow song' is symbolic of unhappiness in love. Emilia and Desdemona's standards of marital fidelity contrast dramatically.

> **QUESTIONS**
>
> 1. What new insight do we gain about Emilia's character in this scene?
> 2. What do we learn about Venetian society in this scene?
> 3. Find three examples of tragic irony in this scene.

ACT V SCENE I

- Iago and Roderigo plot to attack Cassio that night and kill him.
- Roderigo fails to kill Cassio and is himself murdered by Iago.
- Iago tries to implicate Bianca in the attack on Cassio.

Iago's plot fails for the first time in the play in that Cassio is not killed but wounded only.

There are many instances of irony in this scene, all of which surround the character of Iago: he is repeatedly called 'honest' by everyone. When he enters, he holds a light in his hand.

QUESTIONS

1. What reasons does Iago outline for his intention to murder Cassio?

2. What do Roderigo's last words in the play tell us about the nature of Iago?

3. Find three images used in this scene and comment on their function.

ACT V SCENE II

- Othello murders his wife as she lies on their bed. He thinks that he is carrying out an act of divine justice.
- Emilia condemns Othello's action and vindicates Desdemona's honour and loyalty.
- Emilia explains about the origin of the handkerchief.
- Iago stabs Emilia and kills her.
- Othello is filled with remorse and condemns his action as worthy only of punishment by hell fire. He kills himself.
- Iago refuses to speak and explain the reasons for his actions.
- Lodovico laments the deaths and orders Gratiano to take the fortunes of the Moor. Lodovico says that he will inform the Venetian senate about the tragedy.

The opening speech of this scene is a soliloquy rich in images that show us Desdemona's virtue and goodness. Emilia's courage and heroism are evident in her defence of Desdemona throughout this scene and also in her death at the hands of her husband. Othello uses vivid images and poetic language to describe his situation. The enigmatic nature of Iago's wicked operations are evident in the images used about him: a 'devil', 'a viper', 'a damned villain', 'a hellish villain' and 'a Spartan dog'.

QUESTIONS

1. Find three ideas that Othello uses about his wife before he kills her.

2. How does Emilia describe Othello's action?

3. How does Othello describe his character and action in his final speech in the play?

CHARACTER ANALYSIS

OTHELLO

Othello is a Moor living in Venice and he has an important position in the Venetian army as a general. When we first meet him in the play, our impressions are positive. He is called 'the valiant Moor' by the Venetian senate who esteem him highly because of his contribution in helping the state of Venice. From his first words and speeches in the play, we sense that he is a man who has huge powers of self-control. He also appears to come from noble stock: 'I fetch my life and being/From men of royal siege,' he tells Iago calmly when the latter tries to frighten him about Brabantio's anger over Desdemona.

It would seem that A.C. Bradley's assessment of the character of Othello is fitting. Bradley saw Othello as a man who has been steeled by the experience of 'countless perils, hardships and vicissitudes', a man who is able to declare his love for Desdemona quite openly before the entire Venetian senate. At first, we see Othello as a man who is not intimidated by dignitaries nor is he elated by honours. At first, he seems a character who is secure from all dangers without and all rebellion within.

However, as Bradley points out, this impression is shattered early on. The sources of danger for Othello are identified early on in his character: his mind is simple and unobservant and his nature tends outward. He is not introspective and he lacks the capacity to reflect on action. Emotion excites his imagination but it confuses and dulls his intellect. He has little experience of corruption in humankind and he knows little about Venetian women, and Venetian culture in particular:

> Little of this great world can I speak
> More than pertains to feats of broil, and battle.

It seems therefore that Othello is a man of action rather than theories. His experience of life has been limited to the battlefield. He fails to understand Brabantio's position, claiming that 'My services which I have done to the signiory/Shall out tongue his complaints.' They do nothing to placate the grief of a father who has lost his only daughter. But Othello fails to understand this because he lacks insight into human nature.

Othello possesses a sense of control and power and is supreme in situations where everything is objective and calculable. He preserves his supremacy by presuming always that a thing is what it seems to be. He believes Iago's words that 'men should be what they seem'. In wartime, he is able to destroy the enemy without: the observable, calculable, identifiable enemy. In peacetime, he is destroyed by the enemy within: the subtle, intangible, hidden enemy, which is born out of, and thrives on, the confusion between what is and what seems to be.

Othello's basic flaw lies in the narrowness of his intellectual and moral vision, which prevents him from discerning appearance from reality and so gives rise to a profound state of internal insecurity. This, in turn, becomes the seedbed of his poor judgement, his jealousy and his self-pity. An insecure person typically seeks to define their self and to derive a sense of their own worth by establishing bonds with people and forces outside of themselves. Othello does this in the play. He cannot find the basis of order and stability within himself, so he must construct that basis outside. Othello creates stability by constructing his position in public and in private.

In public, Othello establishes his position in society by asserting (in an inordinately self-conscious way) his military prowess.

In private, Othello comes to understand, define and stabilise his selfhood through his relationship with Desdemona. He loves her truly. He sees her as perfect. He unites his whole being to her and he knows that the order of his very existence depends on her. For this reason, he cannot tolerate even the slightest suspicion of wrongdoing on her part:

> But I do love thee, and when I love thee not,
> Chaos is come again.

This is the flawed nature of Othello's love for Desdemona: it is deeply qualified by a concern for the self. It could be said that he is not generous in love – he is selfish. His insecurity is manifested in his awareness of how much he, personally, depends on his own love for Desdemona.

Part of his tragedy lies in the fact that his whole nature seems indisposed towards jealousy; he probably never experienced this emotion in his life. His description of himself as one who is 'not easily jealous but being wrought Perplex'd in the extreme' is quite telling.

When he does begin to experience the stabs of jealousy in Act III, scene iii, he acts rashly and seeks immediate proof in order to resolve all doubt without reflection of any kind.

In addition, he is quite gullible. This means that he becomes an open target for deception. Iago's assessment of him as a man 'who thinks men honest but that seem to be so...And will as tenderly be led by the nose/As asses are' is obviously true. This weakness in his character, together with a misplaced confidence in the 'honesty' of Iago, contributes to his tragic fate.

The breakdown in Othello's self-control begins to occur in Act III, scene iii, or what is commonly known as the 'Temptation Scene'. The insidious poison of Iago's evil insinuations and suggestions work their way through this scene, polluting Othello's faith in his wife's honour and fidelity. This deterioration within Othello is shown in his language patterns and particularly in his use of imagery. He begins to break down under the pressure of the appalling idea that Desdemona, a most pure woman, could have sinned with Cassio. As Othello's intellect deteriorates, his language changes:

> Arise black vengeance...
> Yield up, O love, thy crown and hearted throne
> To tyrannous hate.

It could be said that Othello does not gain any deep insight at the end of the play. He admits at the play's conclusion that he 'lov'd not wisely but too well' but this is not insightful: if anything, he loved himself too well. Perhaps this failure to reach a sufficient level of self-knowledge is his final tragedy. Some critics including T.S. Eliot view Othello as a man who deceives himself and basically is unable to understand the truth underlying his nature and personality. If one were to adopt such a view it is difficult for a reader to take the character of Othello very seriously.

However, the richness of Shakespeare's art enables us to become exposed to a man who embodies many diverse traits of character, and who tragically misuses his freedom and judgement to such a degree that the culminating effect is simply profound catastrophe and suffering for both himself and the people around him.

IAGO

Some critics maintain that the plot of the play is based on the character of Iago in action. This statement is true to a certain extent. The action in the play develops speedily through the intervention of Iago and the fact that he possesses a truly acute and shrewd insight into human nature, both its strengths and weaknesses. In particular, Iago manages to exploit fully the weaknesses of his employer, Othello. Iago exploits Othello to such a degree that real havoc occurs in the play.

Iago is a Venetian soldier whose professional status is quite low on the scale. We learn early on in the first act that Cassio, another Venetian in the army, has been given a higher rank than Iago. Obviously Iago lacks the experience and knowledge of military science and is inferior in ability to Michael Cassio.

It is important to distinguish between Iago's character and his role in the play. Iago's role in the play is made up of many elements. Among them are the following:

- to set the plot in operation
- to wreak havoc on the lives of people (mainly Othello and Desdemona)
- destroys Othello's marriage
- manipulates Roderigo and uses him for his money
- Iago provides a realistic representation of the evil capacity inherent in human nature.

Iago manages to set the plot in operation in many ways. Shakespeare makes use of the soliloquy, whereby he can fabricate his plot and provide reasons for his revenge.

He is a master of intrigue who controls every event and character in the play. He manages to do this through his highly successful assessment of character together with his capacity to manipulate people through language.

Throughout the whole play, Iago dictates the terms of the action. Predominant in him, however, is his need to feel that he is in control. He must be in control of himself and of his world. For Iago, it is clear that the world is a jungle, where relationships consist of hunting or being hunted. Iago sees the world as an environment where only the fittest survive. His assessment of being the fittest involves being the most ruthlessly predatory. The verbs he uses in his soliloquies or in his conversations with Roderigo point in this direction: they refer to hunting, trapping, enfettering, enmeshing and ensnaring.

Part of Iago's role is also to provide a realistic representation of human nature and the villainy that humankind is capable of. Iago is shown to be a very human villain, a man gifted with some very clear strengths but also some very striking defects. He possesses a supreme vitality and is animated by a sinister glitter to his personality. He is able to assess the good qualities in the people around him, e.g. the fact that Desdemona is virtuous and that the love between her and Othello is strong and real. Iago also acknowledges several times that his plot is born from hell and the devil and it is, therefore, foul and evil.

Even though he is animated by a profound hatred of Othello, he tries to find reasons and justification for his actions. Iago mentions two grievances that he has against Othello in the play:

- Othello gave the lieutenancy to Cassio, who was only a theoretician, a man who 'never set a squadron in the field'.
- Othello might have committed adultery with Emilia, 'For that I do suspect the lustful Moor/Hath leap'd into my seat'.

These suspicions prove groundless and soon it becomes apparent that we must look for a more fundamental reason for Iago's behaviour. Quite simply, he hates the Moor. Many times, both in soliloquy and to Rodrigo, he insists on his hatred of (or denies any love for)

Othello. Iago's hatred of Othello is something intrinsic to his nature, needing no external motive. It is, like the jealousy which Emilia speaks about in the play, 'a monster/Begot upon itself, born on itself.'

As the plot of the play unfolds, we witness how Iago's language contains references to religion. He seems to be his own God, making his own rules. The expression used about him towards the conclusion is that he is a 'demi-devil'. This is a perfectly apt description of his sinister and diabolic operations throughout the tragedy.

Like every human being, Iago possesses strengths and weaknesses. Part of the tragedy in this play lies in the fact that he succeeds in using his supreme strengths in the service of evil and manages to wreak havoc in the lives of some of the main protagonists of this play.

Iago is supremely intelligent. In fact, he is probably the most intelligent character in the entire play. He manages to gain control over every event and every person in the play through his powerful intelligence and capacity to judge people and events so astutely. He possesses a deep insight into human nature. He is the one who sees that Othello may be a powerful military general thoroughly capable of defending his country against any enemy, but Othello is also a man who is gullible and foolish, a man who 'will as tenderly be led by the nose.../As asses are.'

It is Iago who understands fully the good and virtuous nature of Desdemona and who sees that he can use this goodness against her and her husband to 'turn her virtue into pitch/ And out of her own goodness make the net/That shall enmesh 'em all.' And this is exactly what he manages to do in this play, with disastrous consequences for all of the characters.

Iago is also a man who possesses huge powers of self-control. He is like an actor creating his own drama and never letting anyone see behind his mask. At no stage does he allow his sympathy, passion or emotions to get the better of him. He maintains a clear head and a strong focus at all times in the play. While luck, fortune, chance and coincidence play a huge part in furthering his plot, it is his own expert manipulation of events and people that really contributes to his power in the play.

His powers of dissimulation and self-control are powerful and striking. He possesses a keen insight into the motivations underlying human nature and cleverly manages to use every opportunity to his advantage. He is a supreme opportunist. He can exploit every situation fully to his advantage and engineer events in such a way that chaos, distrust and discord are rampant around him and yet everyone will still see him as an 'honest' man. Through the figure of Iago, Shakespeare manages to show us how evil can be compatible with exceptional powers of intellect and will.

Part of Iago's success in manipulating people and events lies in the misconception of his personality on the part of everyone else. Each character falls victim to the false assessment that Iago is thoroughly honest. It is this misconception that gives rise to much of the dramatic irony in the play and lays the ground open for the speedy development of his foul plans and plot.

Iago works hard at reinforcing this image in the minds of everyone – especially his employer, Othello. Early on in the drama we hear Iago tell Othello in a bit of playful boasting:

> …in the trade of war I have slain men
> Yet do I hold it very stuff of conscience
> To do no contriv'd murder. I lack iniquity
> Sometimes to do me service.
>
> (Act I, scene ii)

This is an outright lie, but he has just come on stage with Othello, and he is saying this for his general's benefit, posing as the rough and ready but good-hearted soldier. In the same speech, he alludes to having had the opportunity to kill Roderigo – a man who has said evil things about Othello: 'Nine or ten times/I'd thought to have yerk'd him here under the ribs.' It is clear to us that Iago is lying about what he would actually have done. Iago is intent on maintaining his status as a loyal and trustworthy servant. Of course such an image will impress Othello who is a skilful military soldier. Such behaviour reinforces Iago's image of a man who is in control, and who exhibits a profound degree of integrity and honesty of nature throughout.

Early in the play, Othello commends Iago to the Duke of Venice as 'my ancient;/A man he is of honesty and trust'. This reputation for soldierly honesty, to which deceit is absolutely foreign, is the major reason for Iago's powerful control over Othello. And we should not forget that Othello entrusts even his young bride to Iago's care when Othello is sent to Cyprus. Later on, Cassio is duped by Iago's cunning. Iago comforts Cassio's drunken remorse and counsels him to speak to Desdemona and ask her to try and convince Othello to reinstate Cassio as his lieutenant: 'You advise me well…Goodnight honest Iago'.

Desdemona concurs in the prevailing opinion of Iago ('that's an honest fellow'), as does Lodovico in Act V, scene i, when he refers to Iago as 'a very valiant fellow'.

Like every human being, Iago possesses a certain amount of defects in his character. These contribute to building a more realistic portrait of him as a person. Iago's jealousy is a prominent character trait. When the play opens, we witness Iago's professional jealousy of Cassio in his disparaging comments to Roderigo about Cassio's lack of military abilities: 'Mere prattle, without practise/Is all his soldiership.' This professional jealousy shortly changes to sexual jealousy, when he begins to suspect Emilia's fidelity and senses that she may have slept with Othello – a fact which is not borne out in the play's plot.

His jealousy of Emilia is unreasonable: at no stage in the play can we presume that Othello had an affair with her. Iago's jealousy is indeed pervasive. He is jealous of Desdemona's 'goodness', which he proposes to turn into a trap to catch others, and he is especially jealous of her devotion to Othello. He is jealous enough of Cassio to want him killed as he 'hath a daily beauty in his life,/That makes me ugly.'

Iago works off his own jealousy by creating counter jealousies. He arouses the paternal jealousy of Brabantio. He plays on the jealousy of Roderigo by fooling him and using his money lavishly. He announces in one of his soliloquies how his intention is to put the Moor 'into a jealousy so strong/That judgement cannot cure.' And this he does, with enormous success.

Iago is, as we might expect, not merely jealous. With him, jealousy is but one phase of envy. His heart is dominated by a deep hatred for others and in particular for Othello. The play opens on the theme of hatred. Iago tells Roderigo about the nature of his hatred for Othello: 'I do hate him, as I do hell's pains.'

Iago is cynical about human nature, in particular about the nature of love. He repeatedly expresses his contempt for femininity and women. According to his creed, the good qualities of women are merely suitable to 'suckle fools, and chronicle small beer'.

It is possible that at the core of Iago's villainy is a basic cynicism about all humanity. Even though he has proven himself to be a good soldier for years, Iago actually sneers at duty and loyalty. He considers himself to be beyond morality. In fact he seems incapable of any moral feeling. This we learn in Act I, scene i, when he is speaking to Roderigo:

> I follow him [Othello] to serve my turn upon him…You shall mark
> Many a duteous and knee-crooking knave.

His creed is that egoism is rational; conscience and honour are ridiculous and absurd; virtue is a fig; and virtuous women are only fit for menial and demeaning tasks, such as chronicling small beer and suckling fools. Iago possesses an exceptionally high opinion of himself and considers most people to simply be fools who have not yet learned how to serve their own interests correctly.

Samuel Taylor Coleridge provided a critical interpretation of Iago's character that has survived to this day. Coleridge believed that the key to Iago's character was a type of 'motiveless malignity'. Iago is one of the most sardonically witty and egotistical men in all literature – despite being one of literature's most evil men. Yet when all is said and done,

Iago fascinates us. And perhaps this is true because evil that is represented in a powerful manner can somehow hold one powerfully. Certainly, it is a tribute to Shakespeare's genius that despite everything evil that Iago accomplishes, the playwright never lets us forget that Iago is a human being. The passions he expresses are the same as the ones we have: jealousy, anger, capacity for revenge and vindictiveness. However, it is the extreme nature of these passions and the manner in which he uses them to undermine everything good in human nature that separates most of us from Iago.

Iago cannot control an insatiable need to gratify his disappointments with a type of revenge behaviour that is criminal. He has a satanic strain in him and is devoid of all integrity. He is a clever, calculating man, utterly unable to face the reality of his own nature or to grasp the immensity of the chaos for which he is responsible. He finally becomes so poisoned by his own destructive power that he realises that he too is lost, a victim in the very plot he so carefully and malignantly designed.

Ironically, he is destroyed by love – by the very power that he attacks throughout the entire play. Because he has tunnel vision, he misinterprets people at the end. He fails to take the full nature of his wife into account, a wife whom he maligned, abused and exploited repeatedly. Emilia's loyal and steadfast love for Desdemona exposes the full truth of Iago's character. It is Iago's downfall that the changes wrought for the good within Emilia enable her to vindicate the truth and expose the villainy and treachery of her husband at the conclusion.

Emilia's transformation under Desdemona's influence is dramatised in the concluding scene, when with heroic fortitude she gives her life in defending the honour and virtue of her mistress.

CASSIO

Cassio is more important as a plot functionary than an individual in his own right. In order for Iago's intrigue to be successful, someone like Cassio is needed. Cassio is young, handsome and gallant enough to be a plausible cuckold of Othello. As Iago himself says: 'He hath a person and a smooth dispose/To be suspected, framed to make women false…'; 'Besides the knave is handsome, young, and hath all those requisites in him that folly and green minds look after.'

Cassio occupies a midway position between extremes in relation to the two male protagonists in the drama (much like Emilia functions as a midway character between extreme female characters in the play). Cassio has none of Othello's heroic nobility and, equally, none of Iago's 'demi-devil' depravity. He is a kind of 'everyman', the type of individual who in Shakespeare's tragedies is generally destined to be a survivor at the play's end, when the conflict between good and evil has played itself out.

Cassio is a 'decent' individual, a natural charmer, at ease in the company of both men and women, unwilling to hurt and anxious to be liked. It is indeed his very sociability, his desire to be accepted as a 'good fellow' that helps to bring about his downfall in relation to the drinking episode. On the social and professional level, Cassio is a natural 'insider' in Venice, though a native of Florence. He is obviously a gentleman – well educated, polished and refined in manner – and someone socially acceptable to the Venetian establishment. He has aided Othello in relation to the latter's wooing of Desdemona.

Cassio is also somewhat of a social snob, as we see in his unwary and casual condescending attitude. 'Let it not gall your patience, good Iago/That I extend my manners; 'tis my breeding /That gives me this bold show of courtesy,' he tells Iago as he kisses Emilia, Iago's wife. Cassio exposes his snobbery when, ludicrously drunk, he 'pulls rank' on Iago, reminding him that 'the lieutenant's to be saved before the ancient'.

Professionally, it is obvious that Cassio's prospects are bright: he is a new type of career officer, a strategist and theorist, rather than a footslogging practical soldier such as Iago. Iago's bitter comment emphasises this contrast between them:

> That never set a squadron in the field
> Nor the division of a battle knows
> More than a spinster…Mere prattle without practice
> Is all his soldiership.

(Act I, scene i)

Cassio is weak in different ways. Despite knowing that he has 'very poor and unhappy brains for drinking', he allows Iago to persuade him that it will be discourteous to the Cypriot gallants if he fails to join them for a drink. In this, he shows irresponsibility and a failure of soldierly duty. Othello has put Cassio in charge of the watch that night and Cassio, in getting drunk, puts himself at risk for no good reason. Equally, he is weak in his attitude to Bianca. He has been flattered by her infatuation with him but he is ashamed of the continuing relationship with her. It seems probable that he has been trying to break off the liaison with her, as she accuses him of having 'kept a week away' from her. Cassio later says to Iago that he 'must leave her company' but almost immediately afterwards, he confesses that he intends to sup with her that evening. There is evidence that Cassio is a womaniser. Indeed, one of Iago's initial comments on Cassio stresses this weakness. Iago tells us that Cassio is 'a fellow almost damned in a fair wife'.

In spite of his moral fault lines, there is a core of genuine idealism in Cassio. Cassio sees

Desdemona's true worth and always speaks of her with an almost religious reverence. For him, she will remain always 'the divine Desdemona', a lady of 'most blessed condition'. All of Iago's efforts to involve Cassio in his own sexually suggestive comments on Desdemona prove singularly unsuccessful and unproductive.

On the moral level, Cassio can be seen as a foil to Othello. Othello is no womaniser and his speech to the senate at the play's opening makes clear that he could never have been guilty of Cassio's lax irresponsibility when duty called:

> The tyrant custom…Hath made the flinty and steel couch of war
> My thrice driven bed of down: I do agnize
> A natural and prompt alacrity
> I find in hardness.

(Act I, scene iii)

Cassio and Othello are aligned in that they are both duped by Iago. Cassio's assertion that 'I never knew a Florentine more kind and honest' parallels Othello's statement about Iago: 'A man he is of honesty and trust.' Cassio and Othello take Iago at face value because they both share the assumption that men not only 'should be' but are 'what they seem'. It is their common generous openness of nature, their freedom from petty mistrust and suspicion that makes both men easy victims for the deceitful and false Iago. Shakespeare makes clear this parallel duping of Othello and Cassio by Iago. Perhaps Shakespeare was intent on making us understand that it is precisely the best qualities in us that can make us vulnerable to the machinations of evil.

Cassio is cast in the role of true friend; in opposition to Iago, the seeming friend. But in this drama, where appearance triumphs so absolutely over reality, Cassio appears to Othello to be the betrayer. Only at the end of the play are Othello's eyes opened to the truth: too late, he realises how fatally he has misjudged Cassio. Characteristically, the wronged Cassio bears no grudge at having been so maligned: 'General, I never gave you cause.' Although Othello asks for Cassio's pardon, the old comradeship between them can never be restored.

In relation to this issue of friendship, Cassio's role as friend of Othello has an affinity with Emilia's role in relation to Desdemona. However, Emilia and Desdemona have a friendship that is of a different quality, depth and intimacy from that of Cassio and Othello.

Like Othello, Cassio is subjected to a process of temptation by Iago, and like Othello, he fails in the test. Iago is an expert in probing the weaknesses of people and he succeeds with Cassio, just as he does with Othello. Cassio allows himself to become intoxicated with ludicrous ease, and before he knows what has happened, he finds himself stripped of his lieutenancy: 'I love thee Cassio, but never more be officer of mine.'

Like Othello, Cassio succumbs to Iago's temptation but he is never as deeply tainted by evil as Othello is. He remains clear-sighted about his own weakness, while Othello loses all perspective once jealous passion has dislodged reason in him.

The test of Cassio's moral standing lies in his unwavering loyalty to Othello and in his equally unwavering admiration, bordering on reverence, for Desdemona. The one temptation to which Cassio does not succumb is when Iago seeks to involve him in bawdy talk about Desdemona. Cassio shows himself coldly if politely unresponsive to Iago's insinuations that Desdemona is 'sport for Jove' and 'full of game'. Cassio replies: 'Indeed she is a most fresh and delicate creature…an inviting eye…right modest.'

At the play's end, it is the ordinary, unheroic, middle-of-the-road Cassio who not only survives the wreckage around him but also becomes Governor of Cyprus in Othello's place. However, we are given no sense that there will be any triumph for Cassio in this professional advancement. Cassio is too close to the tragedy that has destroyed the hero he had so much admired and the woman he had so honestly revered.

DESDEMONA

Desdemona is represented in this play as a 'heavenly force', the antithesis of Iago the 'hellish villain'. She is a passive victim of Othello's misdirected passion. She represents selfless love in a world of cruel hatred and destructive selfishness. Religious symbols and images are used repeatedly to describe her character and nature: 'Divine Desdemona'; 'the grace of heaven/Before, behind thee, and on every hand/Enwheel thee round.'

Desdemona's first appearance in the play is shown in her courageous and steadfast defence of her love for her husband Othello before the Venetian senate. She has no problem in vindicating her love and loyalty to her husband before these formidable men: 'my heart's subdued/Even to the utmost pleasure of my Lord,' she tells them clearly and sincerely.

This love that she has for Othello remains strong and steadfast right through to the end. The enormous tragedy of the play is shown in Desdemona's words to Othello at the end of the play. Her only sin is the love she bears for Othello.

From the outset of this tragic play, it is clear that Desdemona has an ideal conception of Othello. Her outlook on him is essentially romantic. Her description of her love for Othello before the senate is as revealing as Othello's way of describing his love for her:

That I did love the Moor to live with him…My heart's subdued
Even to the utmost pleasure of my Lord.
I saw Othello's visage in his mind

And to his honours and his valiant parts
Did I my soul and fortunes consecrate…
Let me go with him.

(Act I, scene iii)

This speech is obviously not simply that of a sentimental hero worshipper. The frankness of Desdemona's commitment of herself to Othello is testimony to her courage and her independence of mind. The problem is that there is more to Othello than 'honours' and 'valiant parts' and Desdemona proves quite unable to recognise or acknowledge this possibility: her view of him remains disastrously unshakeable. It is precisely her naively absolutist loyalty and devotion to her ideal Othello that blinds her to the reality of what is happening to him until it is too late.

Desdemona remains a paragon of supreme virtue. At no time in the play does she condemn Othello for his objectionable treatment of her, but instead she repeatedly excuses his behaviour. When he treats her as a prostitute and humiliates her publicly she lays the blame on political affairs of state. She resembles Othello in her inexperience and knowledge of the real corruption within human nature.

Her inexperience ('her green mind') prevents her from understanding the nature of Othello's transformation of character under the wicked and insidious influence of the diabolic Iago. Indeed the whole tragedy stems from her profound depth of virtue: her exceptional degree of goodness, innocence and selfless love, all of which are cruelly exploited by Iago throughout the play and used as a 'net to enmesh all characters'.

For a lot of the play the idea of goodness becomes synonymous with naivety, stupidity and gullibility. Each good character becomes a helpless victim of Iago's devious intrigues. The tragedy demonstrates how Desdemona becomes an ignorant victim of her own essential goodness. Her sincere and humane concern for Cassio's reinstatement are mistakenly interpreted by Othello, who has been corrupted by Iago. This gives rise to the fundamental misunderstanding which governs their relationship from the 'temptation scene' right through to the end of the play.

At one stage, Emilia (a woman experienced in the world of corruption) hints to Desdemona about the fact that Othello may be jealous. Desdemona's reaction is to pray to heaven to 'keep that monster from his mind'.

When Othello comes to a full realisation about what he has done he speaks about the fact that he deserves to be hurled from heaven and roasted in 'hell fire' and he sees Desdemona as a soul in bliss in paradise.

Of course Desdemona, like Othello, errs in ignorance. This ignorance is fatal, as the events show in the play. In the earlier acts she is active, resolute, confident and decisive. It is no wonder that Othello greets her on his arrival in Cyprus as 'My fair warrior'. She has indeed shown herself daring in so many ways: in being ready to elope with Othello, to defend her actions before the senate, to insist on her right to accompany Othello to Cyprus, and finally to challenge his judgement of Cassio. If anything, it is Desdemona's unhesitating self-assurance that makes us feel uneasy about her.

However, from early in Act IV her attitude is radically altered: it is her passivity that is now disturbing. In addition, she shows a failure of tact and understanding in the obstinacy with which she persists in demanding that Cassio be reinstated in his position. She uses a type of emotional blackmail, making Cassio's reinstatement a test of her husband's love for her.

What her approach does is to make Othello acutely aware of her power over him: 'I will refuse you nothing.' Later, under Iago's influence, Othello will take the fact of her intervention as the sign of her having already exerted that power of hers to reject him. Desdemona's perseverance in urging Cassio's suit is both tactless and imperceptive. Even as late as Act IV, scene ii she is still pursuing Cassio's case, stubbornly ignoring how disastrous an effect her pleading has on Othello. Desdemona and Othello are equally blind to the reality behind their reactions in relation to each other.

The issue of the handkerchief only intensifies the misunderstanding between them and deepens Othello's suspicions and doubts even more. Believing she has mislaid the handkerchief, Desdemona lies to Othello about it. Her innocence is obvious to us, but her lie only serves to convince Othello of her falsehood. The lie itself is of less importance than what follows from it. Othello's reaction provokes an ever more urgent need in Desdemona to continue to lie to herself about the implications of Othello's strange behaviour.

When the worldly-wise Emilia asks 'Is not this man jealous?' in response to Othello's stormy exit, Desdemona can only go so far as to admit 'I never saw this before'. She cannot face the truth of the fact that her marriage is collapsing and she concentrates instead on the 'charm' of the handkerchief which she insists accounts for her husband's 'unquietness'. Nevertheless, Desdemona is aware that her advocacy of Cassio must be temporarily abandoned and so she tells him: 'My advocation is not now in tune...You must awhile be patient.'

Desdemona continues for the rest of the play to excuse her husband's behaviour, attributing his anger and distress to different reasons. She tells Emilia:

Something sure of state
Either from Venice, or some unhatched practice
made demonstrable here in Cyprus to him,
Hath puddled his clear spirit.

(Act III, scene iv)

While Othello clings to the idea that their marriage has been a sham from the outset, Desdemona clings with equal tenacity that all must be well with their relationship, though patently this is not the case. From now on, we shall see her involved in self-preservative delusions:

Nay we must think men are not gods
Nor of them look for such observancy
As fits the bridal.

(Act III, scene iv)

It is not until Othello has so far broken with her as to hit her in public that Desdemona's obstinate refusal to face the unbearable truth of her situation begins to falter (Act IV, scene i). It is now no longer possible for her to ignore or deny what he has become. The sudden blow is less important in the physical sense and far more significant psychologically. Her response registers the degree of shock she has experienced, even though she retains her dignity: 'I have not deserved this,' she tells him. As she quietly leaves the room she explains to him: 'I will not stay to offend you.'

This public humiliation of Desdemona by Othello is a turning point in the play's action and in the relationship between the couple. The degree of the deterioration in their marriage has now been exposed to public scrutiny and comment. Astonished and alarmed, Lodovico urges Othello to recall Desdemona, only to hear the husband refer to his wife in terms that would be appropriate to an accomplished Venetian prostitute: 'What would you with her sir?'/'Sir she can turn and turn and yet go on…And she's obedient, as you say,/ Very obedient'.

There follows that extraordinarily painful episode (Act IV, scene ii) where Othello, now committed to his conviction of his wife's guilt, pictures her as a whore in a brothel, with Emilia as a procuress and himself as the client who has purchased his 'turn' with the prostitute of his choice. At this stage Desdemona does not know what she has done wrong. In an innocent and almost childlike manner she turns to Iago for advice asking him:

What shall I do to win my lord again?
Good friend...I know not how I lost him.

(Act IV, scene ii)

Desdemona senses that somehow she is losing her husband but perhaps the 'good' Iago can help her.

Earlier, Desdemona has asked Emilia to lay on her bed their wedding sheets, as if in an effort to recall her original sense of perfect joy in their love. More practically, she sends for the worldly-wise Iago, in the desperate hope that this shrewd and sensible individual may be able to help her. Every word she addresses to Iago is potent evidence of her childlike simplicity and innocence: 'Those that do teach young babes...I am a child at chiding'; 'Am I that name, Iago?'; 'Good friend, go to him; for by the light of heaven/I know not how I lost him...If e'er my will did trespass 'gainst his love.../Comfort foreswear me'; 'I cannot say "whore"/It does abhor me now I speak the word/To do the act that might the addition earn/Not the world's mass of vanity could make me.'

Her act of kneeling before Iago, so like and so unlike that of Othello earlier, is another of those extraordinary mirror-image episodes which so dramatically highlight the play's tragic ironies. The dialogue between Desdemona and Emilia in the 'willow' scene (Act IV, scene iii) is obviously significant in underlining the differences between their characters and attitudes. The contrast between the two women's moral and emotional standpoints has already been emphasised in Act IV, scene ii, when Emilia, her suspicions aroused, wonders whether 'some eternal villain' has not 'devised this slander' against Desdemona. The latter responds: 'If any such there be, heaven pardon him.' Emilia, incapable of sharing Desdemona's generous forgiveness gives vent to a hot-blooded angry outburst: 'A halter pardon him, and hell gnaw his bones!'

In the final scenes there is no clearer index of the change which has come about in Desdemona's life than in the difference between her buoyant confidence in the early acts and her uneasy tone in the concluding scenes. She even senses that her death is imminent. She tells Emilia: 'If I do die before thee, prithee shroud me/In one of these sheets.' Having somehow lost Othello's love, it is as if all her present and future life is lost to her with it. There is a brooding, dark quality in the atmosphere generated by the words of the willow song.

In the final scene, Desdemona awakens from sleep to the nightmare reality of Othello's murderous passion before her. She is terrified by what she reads in his eyes and his demeanour: 'why I should fear I know not./Since guiltiness I know not; but yet I feel I fear.' Bewildered and inarticulate, she has begun to sense that innocence may not protect her,

'But yet I hope, I hope/They do not point on me.' When he speaks of the handkerchief, her straightforward answer comes too late to unsettle his fixed conviction of her guilt: 'No by my life and soul/Send for the man and ask him'; 'Send for him…Let him confess a truth.' When she hears of Cassio's death, in her innocence, she cries out 'Alas! He is betrayed and I undone', a reaction that will simply confirm Othello's belief in her infamy, just as her childish tears will provide further unbearable testimony to his distorted mind: 'O strumpet…weepst thou for him to my face?'

Now thoroughly frightened, Desdemona reacts with the desperation of a panic-stricken child: 'Kill me tomorrow; let me live tonight!…'; 'But half an hour, but while I say one prayer!' As Othello kills her in a kind of cold fury, her final half-smothered cry will merge with Emilia's off stage call: 'My lord, my lord!…my lord, my lord!'

After Othello has admitted Emilia to the bedchamber, we hear Desdemona's voice again, faintly proclaiming her innocence: 'A guiltless death I die'. Emilia's appalled reaction is to ask 'O who has done this deed?' Incredibly, Desdemona speaks these final words: 'Nobody, I myself, farewell:/Commend me to my kind lord. O farewell!'

Since Act IV, Desdemona has continually tried to be loving rather than blaming. When her husband has killed her, her words (which to Othello will appear to be a voice from the dead) unequivocally affirm the constancy, abundance and endless nature of her love for him. She takes Othello's guilt upon herself, insisting that the deed was not a murder, but a kind of innocent suicide.

Desdemona's dying words testify not simply to the strength of her commitment to Othello, but also and perhaps just as significantly, to her sense of the depth of his commitment to her. She cannot see him as other than 'her kind lord' and, realising that she cannot exist without his love, she accepts her own death: 'Nobody, I myself.' It is this underlying emotional truth that gives a positive moral force to her final words.

It should be said in conclusion that, of course, there are other ways of looking at Desdemona and her death. One critic (Ribner) insists that we should see Desdemona's role symbolically, that we should view her as a Christ figure, a representative of Christian love. She appears in opposition to Iago, the dramatic symbol of evil in the play, whose function is to bring about Othello's downfall. By contrast, Desdemona represents the love of Christ for humankind. She stands for self-sacrifice and for redemption. Ribner argues that Desdemona's forgiveness triumphs at the end over the anarchic hatred and jealousy let loose by Iago, and that she brings about Othello's final salvation.

An alternative approach is to be found among those who favour the psychoanalytic approach to Shakespeare's work: these critics see the play as embodying a particular view of the human psyche. From this perspective Othello, as the play's central figure, represents the ego of the psyche. Iago symbolises the criminal id or 'shadow' self of Othello. Desdemona symbolises the protagonist's superego or conscience. When viewed from this perspective, of course, neither Desdemona nor Iago have any real importance in themselves, since each is a mere projection of a single mind.

Whatever approach is adopted, there is no doubt that in the figure of Desdemona Shakespeare has managed to draw an authentic portrait of a woman who knew how to love with all her being, but also whose exceptional degree of virtue contributed to not only her own tragic outcome but that of those closely associated with her.

EMILIA

Emilia is Iago's wife. She is used in the play in different ways. She appears as:

- a pawn to facilitate Iago's plot
- a realistic portrait of character
- a reviewer of Venetian customs and habits
- a moral commentator on character
- a heroine and loyal companion
- a person who exposes the villainy of Iago at the conclusion
- a defender of the truth.

Emilia's first appearance in the play comes when Othello and his retinue arrive in Cyprus to avert the attack by the Turks on the Venetian stronghold there. She is used in the play as an unwitting pawn or a necessary piece of dramatic mechanism to facilitate the plot of her husband Iago.

Iago manages to use his wife in many different ways. He secures a position for her as assistant to Desdemona, a position that will enable Iago to develop his foul plans for Othello. While Emilia is close to Desdemona, she finds a handkerchief that Desdemona has accidentally dropped and mindlessly hands it to Iago, saying:

> my wayward husband hath a hundred times
> Woo'd me to steal it...what he'll do with it
> Heaven knows, not I
> I nothing but to please his fantasy.
>
> (Act III, scene iii)

This type of thoughtless action serves to underline Emilia's essential superficiality of character and inability to see through her husband's devious nature early on in the drama.

She acts without thinking and simply to please her husband.

Emilia is also used to show how Shakespeare can portray character in a vivid and realistic manner. Her blunt and earthy approach to life and men contrasts dramatically with Desdemona's idealistic and innocent vision of life. In Act III scene iv, Emilia speaks to Desdemona about the fact that all men are simply 'stomachs' that 'eat us hungrily' and 'when they are full/They belch us'. This statement is a negative view of marriage and could highlight the type of relationship she has with Iago. Furthermore, it is interesting that in the same scene we get a clear definition of jealousy from Emilia herself: 'It is a monster/Begot upon itself, born on itself.' We are learning from Emilia's conversations that the relationship between her and Iago may be dramatically different from that between Othello and Desdemona.

Emilia is also used in the play to comment on Venetian customs and habits. In Act IV, scene iii, Desdemona and Emilia have a conversation about marital fidelity. Othello's earlier accusations prompt Desdemona to question whether any woman would choose adultery, since in her mind no good could come of such a deed. The worldly-wise Emilia replies with a cynical good humour that losses and gains are relative and that if the end result of adultery were beneficial one might readily justify it: 'Why the wrong is but a wrong i' the world...'tis a wrong in your own world, and you might quickly make it right.'

It becomes quite clear from their conversation that Emilia is thoroughly familiar with men who 'slack their duties' and who 'pour our treasures into foreign laps'. Marriage and the bonds of loyalty are fragile and vulnerable in this society.

Emilia is used by Shakespeare as a commentator on character and action. It is interesting that in spite of the fact that for a lot of the drama Emilia emerges as a mindless and fairly superficial woman, she is not slow to condemn the fact that Othello has called his wife 'whore'. In a scene filled with dramatic irony, Emilia engages in a violent tirade where she vehemently condemns 'the outrageous knave' and 'scurvy fellow' who has 'devised this slander' in front of her husband Iago.

When Emilia realises that it is Othello who has murdered Desdemona, she denounces his action as that of a black devil, telling him that: 'This deed of thine is no more worthy heaven/Than thou wast worthy her.' Her courage grows in strength as she announces that she will bring him to account for his action: 'I'll make thee known/Though I lost twenty lives.'

When Othello begins to doubt his wife's loyalty and honour, he turns to Emilia and interrogates her about his wife's actions. Emilia is not slow to defend Desdemona's honour and virtue, telling Othello in fiery terms that 'If she be not honest, chaste and true,/There's no man happy' (Act IV, scene ii).

From this stage onward, Emilia's role changes. She becomes the means whereby Desdemona's integrity and virtue are openly vindicated before everyone. Her loyalty and courage are shown dramatically in the concluding scene. She declares openly that she is prepared to lose twenty lives in order to protect the honour of Desdemona. And she does lose her life in that action. As she proceeds to disclose the full nature of her husband's devious schemes, she is stabbed by Iago in front of everyone. Her death is heroic and, as she is laid out on the same bed beside Desdemona, she proceeds to sing the willow song, instilling in the minds of all those who are present the idea that Desdemona was 'chaste' and that 'she lov'd thee cruel Moor'. It can therefore be said that Desdemona has had an enormous influence for good on the character of Emilia.

It is clear that Emilia has absolutely no idea about the deeply malignant quality of her husband's nature until the very end of the play. She is an important character in that she plays various roles and emerges as a realistic representation of human nature. Emilia is the one to finally expose the villainy of Iago.

BIANCA

Bianca is a vital part of the representation of womanhood in this play. As a prostitute, she is a marginalised social figure, very much the outsider in Venetian society. Socially, she is at a polar extreme from the aristocratic Desdemona, the social 'insider' and daughter of a Venetian magnifico, who has been brought up in a fashion that will have sheltered her from contact with and knowledge of that precariously unsheltered underworld which is Bianca's milieu. Bianca is also distanced from Emilia. Even though Emilia is not an aristocrat, she is a respectable married woman and part of an upwardly mobile lower-middle class element in Venetian society, aspiring to establishment status.

All three women are involved in the theme of sexual jealousy, which is such a dominant issue in the play, but Bianca's situation contrasts with that of the other women. She herself is jealous in relation to the man she loves, while the other two women are victims of their husbands' jealousy.

Bianca is what Desdemona is supposed by Othello to be. Bianca and Desdemona provide an interesting contrast in terms of appearances and reality, which is one of the dominant elements in this play.

Desdemona cannot even bear to repeat the name that Othello has used of her, the name that defines Bianca:

I cannot say 'whore'
It does abhor me now I speak the word

To do the act that might the addition earn
Not the world's mass of vanity could make me.

(Act IV, scene ii)

On the level of plot, and how it functions in the play, all three women are involved with the handkerchief as a result of Iago's manipulation of them.

There are some elements of the stereotype in Bianca's depiction: she rants and raves in a vulgar and strident fashion when angered, as prostitutes were deemed to do in that the time: 'A likely piece of work that you should find it in your chamber,' she vociferously protests to Cassio. She works herself up into a fine rage as she gives vent to her jealousy and her sense of being exploited, berating him furiously: 'This is some minx's token, and I must take out the work, there...'

However, Bianca is no mere stereotype. She is genuinely in love with Cassio. It is Iago who comments cynically on the irony of the fact that the prostitute Bianca has fallen for one of her clients:

...a creature
That dotes on Cassio, as 'tis the strumpets' plague
To beguile many and be beguil'd by one.

(Act IV, scene i)

Although Bianca is usually played on the stage as a typical harlot (flaunting her sexuality one moment, raucously angry the next) she is, nevertheless, not so different from the other women in terms of their emotional experience.

Like the other two women, she is emotionally bound to the man she loves and precisely because she loves Cassio, she gives him the power to hurt her, to make her feel rejected and humiliated. In this way, her position is parallel to that of the other women and parallel too, interestingly enough, to that of Othello in relation to Desdemona. When Bianca says resignedly on parting from Cassio in Act III, scene iv, 'I must be circumstanc'd', she is clearly speaking for all the women who figure in the male-dominated world of this drama, giving voice to their enforced acceptance of what they cannot alter, while at the same time, acknowledging their need to be loved.

The theme of appearances and reality is constantly highlighted in relation to the depiction of each woman in the play. Bianca is the reality of the 'strumpet' and the 'whore' that Othello accuses Desdemona of being. The ugliness of the brothel episode in Act IV, where Othello treats Desdemona as 'the subtle whore of Venice' that he believes her to be, sufficiently underlines the sordidness of the prostitute's lifestyle. Cassio's fear of being found in public in company with Bianca: 'I would not have him see me woman'd', makes plain enough the fact that he was ashamed of this liaison, however flattering he found it that Bianca was in love with him.

Later, in an episode contrived by Iago (Act IV, scene i), Cassio talks of Bianca while the watching Othello imagines him to be speaking of Desdemona. We witness here the casual cruelty of Cassio's attitude to a woman whom he sees only as a sexual object and plaything:

> She haunts me in every place…
> thither comes this bauble, by this hand she falls thus about my neck…
> So hangs, and lolls, and weeps upon me…
>
> (Act IV, scene i) ˙

Cassio is incredulous at the idea that anyone could imagine, even for a moment, that he might be so foolish as to consider marrying her: 'What? A customer? I prithee bear some charity to my wit.' Obviously he is aware that he must break up with her, but up to this, he has been too weak and too self-indulgent to do so: 'Well, I must leave her company.'

This episode underlines the scorn with which the prostitute was regarded by the males who exploited her. Bianca's social outcast status is again highlighted when Iago seizes the opportunity to try to incriminate Bianca in relation to Cassio's wounding: 'Gentlemen all, I do suspect this trash/To be a party to this injury…' He is obviously relying on the fact that few will be prepared to believe anything Bianca says in her own defence. The parallel with the falsely accused Desdemona is obvious: Othello will believe nothing that can be said in favour of Desdemona, either by herself or by Emilia, because he is convinced that she is a whore and as such, one to whom lying is second nature and taken for granted.

It is not simply males, however, who scorn and distrust Bianca because of her profession; the 'respectable' Emilia is equally ready to upbraid her: 'Fie, fie upon thee, strumpet'. Here, Emilia is furious because Bianca has dared to address her as though she were her social and moral equal.

Shakespeare makes it clear that Bianca's love of Cassio is sincere. This sincerity is evident in Bianca's last appearance on the stage, when the strength of her feeling makes her forgetful enough of her own safety to rush to him when she sees him wounded. Clearly her pallor is not, as Iago suggests, the result of fear and guilt, but is rather the product of her anxiety for the man she loves.

Both Desdemona and Emilia die defending their own versions of a love that transcends self and selfish considerations. Bianca lives on, but her survival has its own hint of tragedy, since the object of her love will obviously have no further use for what she has to offer him. She is not even present at the play's close.

Bianca, Desdemona and Emilia are all a part of the play's dramatic design and what they represent in the play's world is an essential element in its tragic import.

RODERIGO

Roderigo is described in the stage directions as a 'gulled gentleman'. It is obvious that Roderigo has a lot of money and he is content to hand it over to Iago in the hope that this will secure Desdemona's affections.

Roderigo functions as a dupe or a gullible man who is manipulated repeatedly by Iago in the play and who is used to further his malicious plot. Roderigo's appearance in the opening scene serves several functions:

- Through Roderigo we learn that Iago is not all he seems to be and that he is simply using Othello to 'serve my turn upon him'.
- Roderigo is also used by Iago to rouse Brabantio from his sleep and inform him that his daughter Desdemona has eloped with Othello.

In Cyprus, Iago makes use of Roderigo to vent his disgust and cynicism about love and virtue: 'a fig', love is merely 'a lust of the blood' and marriage a 'frail vow betwixt an erring barbarian and a super-subtle Venetian'. Iago speaks about his attitude to Roderigo in his soliloquies. He considers him a 'snipe' and a 'fool', the 'trash of Venice' whom he is using only for his money.

Iago manipulates Roderigo into provoking a fight with the drunken Cassio. Towards the end of the play we learn from Roderigo's conversation with Iago that he has given him all his jewels and received nothing in return.

Roderigo is a morally weak man who allows himself to be duped into a plot to murder Cassio in the false hope of winning Desdemona's hand in marriage.

In the end, Iago decides to kill Roderigo. Iago is forced to face the fact that he owes Roderigo a large amount of jewels and money and will never manage to pay him. Iago slays him under the pretence of administering justice to Cassio.

Roderigo's last words are chillingly true: 'damn'd Iago, inhuman dog'.

THEMES IN THE PLAY

There are many different themes developed in the play, a selection of which are dealt with in this chapter.

- Dissimulation
- Jealousy
- Racial prejudice
- Women
- Reputation
- Justice

DISSIMULATION

Dissimulation involves concealing the truth by presenting a false image. Dissimulation, deception and false appearances are dominant themes in the play and they are embodied in the character of Iago. Early on, Iago uses these words to describe himself: 'I am not what I am'. This makes clear to us how Iago will operate as the supreme dissimulator in the play.

A lot of his power rests on the fact that everyone mistakenly believes that he is honest. This misconception of his character enables him to use every situation to his advantage and thus bring about his foul plot to cause the ultimate tragedy of the play.

From the outset, Othello blindly trusts Iago. Othello believes fully that Iago is a 'man of honesty and trust'. Othello entrusts the care of Desdemona into the hands of Iago while they are engaged in political affairs in Cyprus. This enables Iago to concoct his scheme to undermine Othello's faith in his wife's fidelity and purity.

At every stage in the plot, Iago's plans flourish and his capacity as supreme dissembler grows. He takes a great delight in this role – this can be seen from the numerous soliloquies in which he talks about other characters and makes clear just how much he despises them. He calls Othello a fool who 'thinks men honest that but seem to be so'. All the characters fall victim to Iago's capacity to deceive and play a false part. Everyone is fascinated by the external glitter to his character, not realising that underneath lies a deeply diabolic and sinister nature that is thoroughly operating in the service of evildoing.

When Cassio is dismissed from his position as lieutenant after being duped by Iago, the first person he turns to for help and advice is Iago himself! Cassio repeatedly speaks about 'honest Iago' and about the fact that he 'never knew a Florentine more kind and honest'.

Of course, this situation is used opportunely by the villainous Iago, who advises Cassio to intercede with Desdemona, telling him that the 'virtuous Desdemona' will certainly 'help to put you in your place again'. Underlying Iago's intentions is his vicious plot to use Desdemona's virtue in order to make her goodness a net that will trap all the characters that he despises.

Iago handles every situation that crops up in the play with a tremendous skill and dexterity. He deftly deceives every person: Othello, Desdemona, Roderigo, Cassio and even his own wife, Emilia. He manipulates every character in the play with a cynicism and ironic contempt, and speedily turns everything to his own advantage. Even rather mild scenarios become dangerous when Iago is involved. On the night that he succeeds in getting Cassio drunk, Iago cleverly plants the seeds of doubt within Montano the Governor of Cyprus about Cassio's capacity for alcohol: 'He'll watch the horologe a double set/If drink rock not his cradle.' Of course, Iago knows that this seed of doubt about Cassio's virtue will undermine Cassio's reputation and can be used later on to consolidate Iago's plot even more.

Shakespeare manages to show us how this issue of dissimulation can coexist with outstanding human powers and strengths. Iago's human qualities are exceptional and powerful. He possesses a strong sense of self-control – at no stage does he allow himself to be intimidated or daunted by fear of what other people might do or think about him. Even when Othello, carried away by passion, actually attacks Iago physically in asking him for proof that Desdemona has committed adultery, Iago remains unshaken. In this scene, he calmly plays up on his own reputation for honesty, telling Othello in hurt tones that he, Iago, is a:

> O…wretched fool
> That livest to make thine honesty a vice...
> O world
> To be direct and honest is not safe.
>
> (Act III, scene iii)

The fact that Iago is probably the most intelligent of all the people in the play enables him to sustain this deception and manipulation so successfully. There are many different factors that facilitate his powers of dissimulation. He seems to be an expert in summing up each of the different characters he encounters. He easily assesses their nature, both for good and evil. He realises that Othello possesses certain flaws that can be used against him. In a long soliloquy, Iago speaks about how 'the Moor' has 'a free and open nature...' and 'will as tenderly be led by the nose.../As asses are'. Iago readily exploits the gullible Othello and manipulates him to his own advantage. He uses Desdemona's pure and unadulterated virtue to further his own evil schemes.

Iago's capacity to deceive extends even to his own wife, Emilia. At no stage is Emilia aware of the depths of evil inherent in her husband's real nature. Even though she is a realist who knows fully the corrupt ways of the world, when the truth of her husband's actions becomes exposed, she is astounded. She cannot believe the fact that his nature would have descended to such depths of evil. She challenges him:

> Disprove this villain …
> He says thou told'st him that his wife was false
> I know thou did'st not: Thou'rt not such a villain
> Speak for my heart is full.
>
> (Act V, scene ii)

Shakespeare uses irony to dramatise this theme of dissimulation. Irony is an ideal technique to project such a theme, involving as it does the discrepancy between what is said or implied and what is really the case. The root of much of the irony in this play lies in the basic misconception by everyone that Iago is 'honest'.

And so a network of ironies – from situational, to dramatic to verbal – illustrates this theme. In Act IV scene ii, when Emilia speaks to her husband about how Othello has mistreated Desdemona, the encounter is rich with irony. She claims that:

> The Moor's abused by some outrageous knave,
> Some base notorious knave, some scurvy fellow.
>
> (Act IV, scene ii)

The play abounds in similar examples of the clever use of irony. Shortly after Iago has managed to destroy Cassio's reputation by tempting him to get drunk and provoking him to fight, Othello in anger turns to his ensign in order to get the truth about the incident. Here, in front of everyone gathered in the citadel in Cyprus, Iago manages to manifest an extraordinary degree of control. He gives the appearance of a man who feels a strong sense of misgiving for betraying Cassio and yet must show loyalty to his master by telling the truth. Of course the 'truth' he tells ensures that Cassio is immediately dismissed from his position as lieutenant.

Iago's ability to deceive everyone causes havoc as the events of this drama unfold and the conflict intensifies. It is only when Othello has murdered his wife that the full reality underlying Iago's plausible appearance of honesty is finally and ultimately cracked. His smooth veneer of honesty and integrity is stripped bare by Emilia's staunch defence of the truth and her fearless denunciation of his villainy.

Shakespeare has managed to draw a powerful picture of dissimulation in the figure of the leading protagonist in the play. He is a man endowed with outstanding talents and strengths but who tragically uses them in the service of evildoing. The use of irony to outline this theme contributes to the dramatic power of this tragic play.

RACIAL PREJUDICE

As a Moor from another culture, Othello is an outsider in this society and hence he is regarded with suspicion and distrust. His position as a stranger to this culture intensifies his vulnerability and actually facilitates Iago's devious plot.

From the opening scene, we are confronted with the particular issue of racial prejudice. Iago's resentment and spite rouses Roderigo who, in turn, provokes the superstitious Brabantio with the words:

> an old black ram, is tupping your white ewe...
> Your fair daughter…transported…to the gross clasps of a lascivious Moor...
>
> (Act I, scene i)

Later on that night, when Brabantio takes up the issue in the Venetian Senate, he condemns Othello for having 'abused her delicate youth with foul charms' (Act I, scene ii).

This attack is directed at Othello. In the words of Brabantio, Othello has bewitched Desdemona to such a degree that 'she ran from her guardage to the sooty bosom of such a thing as thou' (Act I scene ii).

Prior to this, Brabantio entertained Othello in his house, paying tribute to him as a high ranking military general. However, the marriage of his beloved daughter to this Moor, this outsider, is an entirely different matter. It actually leads him to say to Roderigo, who he really despises: 'O, that you had had her' (Act I ,scene i).

Othello is deeply insecure because he lacks real-life knowledge of issues such as marriage, social relations between men and women, and certain customs and traditions peculiar to Venice. It is this lack of knowledge and experience that leaves him an open target for exploitation. Iago's words in the 'temptation scene' are telling in this regard: 'In Venice they do not let God see the pranks,/They dare not show their husbands' (Act III, scene iii).

Subtly wrangling his perverted mind into Othello's weak nature, Iago suggests in Act III, scene iii, that perhaps the cause of Desdemona's infidelity has to do with race and colour:

Ay, there's the point: as, to be bold with you,
Not to affect many proposed matches,
Of her own clime, complexion, and degree…
We may smell in such a will most rank,
Foul disproportion; thoughts unnatural…
I may fear/Her will recoiling to her better judgement
May fall to match you with her country forms
And happily repent.

(Act III, scene iii)

That Iago succeeds in undermining Othello's faith in himself and in Desdemona becomes saliently clear from the soliloquy that follows immediately after the above lines.

It is Othello himself who articulates in Act III, scene iii, how vulnerable and how defenceless he is because of his colour.

Haply, for I am black
And have not those soft parts of conversation
That chamberers have…

(Act III, scene iii)

His tragedy lies in the fact that he is unable to transcend these limitations within his own nature and arrive at the real truth. Instead, he consolidates his weaknesses even more by acting on impulse and executing judgement on Desdemona.

There is no doubt that the issue of racism and the underlying prejudice generated by it contributes to precipitating a good deal of the tragedy in this play.

WOMEN

All the female characters are unwitting victims of deception, guile and intrigue. They all inadvertently act as instruments of evil. Take for instance Bianca's affair with Cassio or Emilia's thoughtlessness in handing over the handkerchief to Iago, which furnishes him with proof of Desdemona's 'infidelity'. There is also the fact that Desdemona cannot discern the capacity within human nature for corruption and possesses a totally pure and idealistic vision of the human being. There is a striking contrast drawn throughout the play between the characters of Desdemona and Emilia. Desdemona's moral rectitude is integral, inviolate and pure. Emilia on the other hand is more worldly, her moral reasoning in the face of infidelity is tenuous and weak. She would 'venture Purgatory to make her husband a monarch'.

The conversation between Desdemona and Emilia about marital infidelity (Act IV, scene iii) serves the function of confirming and consolidating Desdemona's absolute integrity in the eyes of Emilia. This scene also functions to contrast the different standards of values professed by both women. Emilia has weaker moral standards, standards which are corruptible and more worldly. For this reason, it is fitting that Emilia becomes the woman to stand up and vindicate the purity and integrity of Desdemona's virtue when her husband has murdered her. Emilia's defence of Desdemona's innocence and purity sounds authentic and realistic, spoken as it is by a woman who knows the ways of the world thoroughly.

It is ironic that Emilia becomes the one to expose the villainy of Iago. Despised repeatedly by her husband for being a strumpet, she emerges at the conclusion of this tragedy as a heroine who upholds truth and honour. It is through Emilia's love and loyalty to Desdemona that the powers in Venice become aware of Iago's wicked and evil operations. These were two virtues that Iago tried to erode steadily in the drama and they end up destroying him at the end.

The general idea left to us in the play is that 'women must be circumstanc'd', meaning they live in a society where they are expected to just put up with the state of affairs while, on the other hand, men can do what they like.

JEALOUSY

This is an issue that permeates much of the play. There are overtones of jealousy in the opening lines. These stem from the jealous references and disparaging comments that Iago makes about the character of Cassio:

> A fellow almost damn'd in a fair wife,
> That never set a squadron in a field,
> Nor the division of a battle knows,
> More than a spinster...
> Mere prattle without practise
> Is all his soldiership.
> (Act I, scene i)

The root of Iago's envy is his anger at Cassio's military expertise and the fact that Cassio has been promoted ahead of him. Iago's jealousy is pervasive. He himself acknowledges that he is jealous of Cassio:

He has a daily beauty in his life
That makes me ugly
(Act V, scene i)

Iago works off this jealousy by creating counter jealousies. Othello becomes his primary target. Iago announces in an early soliloquy:

I will put the Moor
At least, into a jealousy so strong,
That judgement cannot cure
(Act II, scene ii)

Iago manages to achieve this with consummate success. Othello's dying words confirm the truth of this and the success of Iago's warped intrigues:

Speak of me...
Of one not easily jealous, but being wrought
Perplex'd in the extreme...
(Act V, scene ii)

It is clear that Othello's nature is normally indisposed towards jealousy or envy of any kind. So once it dominates him, it consumes and utterly destroys him. The disposition of his temperament is to act rashly and impulsively, to seek immediate proof and resolve his doubts without stopping to reflect on the consequences of his actions. Of course, Iago perceives all this thoroughly. Halfway through the 'temptation scene', when he is handed the handkerchief, Iago is able to assess fully the state of Othello's inner nature:

...trifles light as air
Are to the jealous, confirmations strong
As proofs of Holy Writ
(Act III, scene iii)

Iago appraises completely that Othello's soul is animated by an uncontrolled ,'unbookish jealousy'. It is perhaps significant that it is both Emilia and Iago who provide us with a definition of jealousy in the play.

Iago warns Othello to be wary of jealousy in the 'temptation scene':

O, beware, my lord of jealousy!
It is the green-ey'd monster, which doth mock
The meat it feeds on

(Act III, scene iii)

And later on Emilia tells Desdemona that Othello's ill-treatment of her may be due to jealousy and proceeds to echo Iago's earlier words,

...It is a monster
Begot upon itself, born on itself

(Act II, scene iv)

The fact that both characters – Iago and Emilia – offer a clear definition of jealousy at different stages in this play could be an indication that they have experience of this vice from their marriage.

Within the context of this play and the ensuing events, jealousy does turn out to be a monster that breeds on itself, an evil that is self-destructive in the lives of people.

The conclusion of the play dramatises this point vividly. Othello destroys the bonds of his marriage, the beautiful Desdemona and then kills himself. However, Iago's destructive plot is overturned and his devilry unmasked at the conclusion.

REPUTATION

The theme of reputation is intertwined with the themes of honour, social status and self-esteem in the play. Our notion of reputation is bound up with other people's opinions of us. This links to the notion of self-image, a theme that is crucial to the play.

The setting of the play is a male-dominated and military world where considerations about promotion, career achievement, honour, loyalty to the state, courage and heroism are considered 'manly' behaviour both on and off the battlefield. It follows, therefore, that if one feels injured in one's reputation one is likely to suffer a crisis of identity. This obsession with the manner in which others see us applies to all the leading male characters in the play.

When Cassio is dismissed on account of his drunken brawl he is chiefly concerned that he has suffered a public disgrace. He fears that he has let himself down before others and has lost his position as lieutenant:

Reputation, reputation, reputation! O I have lost my reputation.
I have lost the immortal part of myself, and what remains is bestial.

(Act II, scene iii)

This histrionic response is not intended to be taken seriously by us. His reaction is essentially superficial. However, Cassio's reaction is not unlike that of Othello later when he imagines that Desdemona has betrayed him:

> O farewell the plum'd troop and the big wars
> That make ambition virtue…
> Farewell Othello's occupation's gone.
> > (Act III, scene iii)

Othello can no longer find meaning in the soldier's life, because his good name has been besmirched with his wife's loss of reputation:

> My name that was as fresh
> As Dian's visage, is now begrim'd and black
> As mine own face
> > (Act II, scene iii)

We gain some interesting insights into this theme of reputation through the figure of Iago. He constantly tailors his comments to fit the occasion and the individual he is addressing. In his guise of comforter and friend, he counsels the grieving Cassio and tells him that:

> …reputation is an idle and most false
> imposition oft got without
> merit and lost without deserving;
> You have lost no reputation at all,
> unless you repute yourself such a loser.
> > (Act II, scene iii)

Later, however, he will speak very differently to Othello on this issue:

> Good name in man and woman, dear my lord;
> Is the immediate jewel of their souls:
> Who steals my purse steals trash
> 'tis something, nothing…
> But he that filches from me my good name
> Robs me of that which not enriches him
> And makes me poor indeed.
> > (Act III, scene iii)

In reality, Iago is obsessed with the notion of reputation. He is an extraordinarily vain man. He has suffered a public humiliation at Othello's hands, in having been passed over for promotion in favour of the 'mere arithmetician' Cassio. His furious resentment at his 'loss of face' among his fellow officers in the Venetian army is obvious in his envenomed words to Roderigo at the beginning of the play:

> I know my price, I am worth no worse a place
> But he, as loving his own pride and purposes...
> Nonsuits my mediators.
> (Act I, scene i)

It is this 'loss of face' that in the first place explains Iago's hatred of both Othello and Cassio and his desire to make them both suffer a similar loss of status and honour.

Iago is also concerned with reputation in another sense. In this male-dominated world the subject of reputation in sexual matters is a primary consideration. The cuckolded husband was a farcical figure, a pathetic object, a fit subject for the scornful jests of his fellows. The ultimate humiliation for a man in this society was to find himself betrayed by his wife.

Iago chooses to imagine that he has been so dishonoured by Othello and even by Cassio. In both cases, the loss, or imagined loss of reputation, is enough to motivate Iago's vengeful plot:

> It is thought abroad that 'twixt my sheets
> He's done my office, I know not if't be true...
> Yet I, for mere suspicion in that kind
> Will do, as if for surety:
> (Act I, scene iii)

Iago is not just content to have Cassio dismissed but Othello must be brought down to Iago's own 'dishonoured' level:

> even with him wife, for wife:
> Or failing so, yet that I put the Moor,
> At least, into a jealousy so strong
> That judgement cannot cure;
> (Act I, scene i)

Iago then is obsessed with the manner in which he appears to others. Even his passing comment on the 'daily beauty' in Cassio's life that 'makes me ugly', is testimony to this obsession.

Iago also rests on his reputation for honesty and uses this to a supreme advantage in the play in order to bring his wicked plot to fruition. Iago gloats in the reputation he has earned for himself, which is based on appearance alone. 'I am not what I am,' he tells Roderigo early on in the play. Iago delights in the ease with which he fools others, 'as honest as I am'.

Initially, Othello has no need for self-analysis nor does he fear the opinion of others. When Iago suggests that he should hide himself before the wrath of Brabantio, Othello forcefully declares:

> I must be found...
> My parts, my title and my perfect soul
> Shall manifest me rightly.
> > (Act I, scene ii)

He is supremely confident of his own integrity and his contribution to Venetian government.

However, once Iago begins to work on Othello and forces him to reassess his position, Othello begins to become obsessed with the issue of reputation and self-image. Iago convinces Othello that his male honour has been humiliated by Desdemona's infidelity. Othello's reaction to the supposed betrayal is a mixture of outraged pride and bitter humiliation. He states that he could have borne anything except the misery of having become

> A fixed figure for the time of scorn
> To point his slow and moving finger at.
> > (Act IV, scene ii)

This attitude stems from the prevailing value system which asserted that a wife was the 'property' of her husband. If Desdemona is adulterous, she has not simply dishonoured herself but, far more significantly, she has dishonoured and shamed her husband. Once Othello is convinced of Desdemona's infidelity, he regards her not as a woman who has committed a single transgression, but as a whore. She is 'that subtle whore of Venice that married with Othello' (Act IV, scene ii).

As such, she is dishonest, unchaste and a woman of ill repute who has disgraced her husband and is entitled to public humiliation. That is why Othello strikes her publicly and calls her a whore repeatedly. She has lost her reputation and honour and is simply fit to be despised.

When Othello realises too late that he has erred in murdering his wife, he seeks to salvage some of his reputation. When he kills himself he believes that he is still Othello who 'has done the state some service'. In carrying out his final act as Governor of Cyprus, he still wishes to be the defender of Venice and its civilised values. At the same time, he believes that his reputation of the past is gone forever: 'That's he that was Othello. Here I am' (Act V, scene ii).

Emilia's attitude to the subject of reputation is complex. At one stage she seems the respectable married woman, who is outraged by the prostitute Bianca's effort to suggest that she herself is as 'honest' as Iago's wife. However, Emilia's private approach to 'sexual politics' is worldly, cynical and resigned to the reality of male dominance. She is also clear-eyed about the dubious double standards of her world.

In discussing the subject of adultery with Desdemona, she half-jokingly suggests that one might cuckold one's husband if one could get away with it 'in the dark', and after all 'who would not make her husband a cuckold to make him a monarch'? More seriously, she adds that wives learn to do 'ill' by their husbands' bad example.

Despite her cynical worldliness, Emilia recognises in Desdemona a quality so fine and so rare that she cannot endure to keep silent when Othello, having murdered his wife, proceeds to justify his deed by defaming her. In a mood of total transcendence, Emilia endorses Desdemona's reputation, defending her mistress's good name with her life:

> Moor, she was chaste, she loved thee, cruel Moor
> So come my soul to bliss as I speak true;
> So speaking as I think, I die, I die.
>
> (Act V, scene ii)

Shakespeare has managed to show how the issue of reputation and honour in the male-dominated world of the play has many different aspects and is an important part of the motivations underlying many of the leading protagonists.

JUSTICE

The theme of justice can be seen throughout the entire action of the play. Justice means to give every person what is due to them. It is, therefore, associated with a sense of right and wrong, with the pronunciation of a verdict or the delivery of a sentence. Justice is also concerned with upholding the law and maintaining order and harmony.

The Venetian Signory or Council Chamber symbolises this sense of ordered Renaissance civilisation. Here the Duke presides over law cases and here Brabantio, having attempted to make a 'citizen's arrest', comes to arraign Othello, since he believes that Othello has seduced Desdemona by unlawful means in order to elope. The Duke listens to both sides in what is, in fact, a legal trial. Brabantio speaks as a prosecuting attorney and also as witness for the prosecution, while Othello conducts his own defence, calling on Desdemona to act as his witness. In the end, the Duke delivers his carefully considered judgement in Othello's favour.

The same approach to justice is found in Act II, scene III, when Othello (as governor of Cyprus) pronounces judgement on the drunken Cassio and metes out punishment to him in the form of 'cashiering'. Cassio is dismissed from his position as lieutenant. The fact is, however, that Othello's was a less considered judgement than that of the Duke earlier: Othello has listened to one side of the argument only.

The 'brothel' episode in Act IV, scene II, is also relevant in terms of this theme of justice. Here Othello acts as interrogator in a legal trial, cross-examining Emilia in relation to the accused Desdemona. Despite Emilia's robust efforts to defend her mistress and Desdemona's own impassioned cry of innocence, Othello judges his wife to be guilty.

Later on in the play, when Othello swears a solemn oath (by 'Yond marble heaven') to take Desdemona's life, he claims that he is doing so in the name of justice. It is clear to us that he actually seeks revenge for the imagined cuckolding. 'I'll chop her into messes! Cuckold me!' he exclaims, revealing his true motivations.

His ready agreement to Iago's suggestion that he strangle Desdemona in their marriage bed (the marriage bed that her supposed lust has desecrated) is an example of that false travesty of justice which is essentially a return to barbarism: 'Good, Good, the justice of it pleases'. In each case, what these men seek is retribution for the sexual humiliation they perceive themselves to have suffered.

In the concluding scene of the play, Othello enters the bed chamber in a mood of high-wrought solemnity, which is essentially grotesque. As he acts out his role of judge, priest and executioner, he speaks in measured tones, about what he sees as a pagan ritualised sacrifice: 'It is the cause, it is the cause…' In this speech, Othello seeks to solemnise what is a barbaric act, and thereby control his own response to the real horror of what he is about to do. That effort at control, of course, breaks down in the face of Desdemona's frantic efforts to dissuade him: the false pose of self-sacrificing duty in the name of justice is exposed for what it is:

Yet she must die, else she'll betray more men…;
O perjur'd woman! thou dost stone thy heart
And makest me call what I intend to do
A murder, which I thought a sacrifice.

(Act V, scene ii)

Othello kills Desdemona in an ugly burst of frenzy and the issue of justice re-emerges at the play's conclusion where Othello makes a last 'speech from the dock'. It is a kind of epitaph on himself: 'Nothing extenuate, nor set down aught in malice…'

He then proceeds to exercise justice as he had once carried out justice in the case of the 'malignant Turk' in Aleppo. In realising that he has murdered his innocent wife, he now visualises himself as traitor and enemy of Venice, a man who has betrayed his Christian faith and trust as Governor of Cyprus. He is no longer the guardian of civilised values. He makes the accusation towards himself, condemns himself to hell and executes himself.

In her last breath, Desdemona sought to exonerate Othello. Before he dies Othello visualises her as a spirit of heavenly retributive justice:

This look of thine will hurl my soul from heaven
And fiends will snatch at it.

(Act V, scene ii)

Othello believes that in his death he will have purged the evil within himself and righted the balance in favour of order, stability and moral rectitude.

Shakespeare brings his play to a conclusion with the arrest of Iago. Lodovico announces that Montano the Governor of Cyprus will be the one who will inflict punishment on Iago. Justice will be meted out to the villain of the play, and a certain sense of order and harmony is restored at the conclusion.

LANGUAGE AND IMAGERY

The use of imagery in this play fulfils three purposes:
- It creates a particular atmosphere through building up the setting and background.
- It outlines the 'tone' of a character's outlook, mindset and value system.
- It highlights certain issues that are important in the play.

ATMOSPHERE

Storm Imagery

In this play, the waves are seen as mountainous, the troughs as valleys and the intermingling of sea and sky 'the great contention of the sea and skies'. All of these images suggest confusion and danger, just like the treacherous 'Tempests...high seas...howling winds... gutter'd rocks' threaten to destroy ships. This imagery reaches its height in Othello's words on his reunification with Desdemona:

> If after every tempest come such calms
> May the winds blow, till they have waken'd death
> And let the labouring bark climb hills of seas
> Olympus-high...'
>
> (Act II, scene i)

Colour Imagery

There are constant references to blackness and whiteness, evoking the struggle between good and evil throughout the play. Note the references to Othello as an 'old black ram' and Desdemona as the 'white ewe'. The Duke of Venice speaks to Brabantio about Othello, saying: 'Your son-in-law is far more fair than black'. Iago plans to turn Desdemona's virtue into 'pitch'. Othello refers to Desdemona's reputation becoming 'begrimed and black as mine own face'. In the final scene, Othello's words stress the whiteness of Desdemona's skin as an aspect of her physical beauty:

> Nor scar that whiter skin of hers than snow,
> And smooth as monumental alabaster
>
> (Act V, scene ii)

Finally, there is Othello's anguished reference to Desdemona's pallor 'Pale as thy smock'. This is a reminder to us of her innocence and it is linked also with Othello's later realisation of that angelic innocence of hers, whose look will cast him into hell. Colour imagery is often used also to refer to heaven and hell. Later in the play, Othello speaks about Desdemona as a devil:

> Furnish me with some swift means of death
> For the fair devil.
>
> (Act III, scene iii)

CHARACTER

Imagery also serves the function of creating the 'tone' of a character's mind, outlook and value system. This is particularly relevant in the case of Othello and Iago. At the beginning of the play, each of these men uses a pattern of imagery that contrasts dramatically with that of the other man. The contrasting imagery is used to show us the contrasts in how each man views the world and the people who inhabit it. In general, Iago's image system projects a view of humanity as petty, debased, ugly and animalistic. This is in keeping with his negatively cynical outlook. He regards Othello as an 'ass', Roderigo as a 'snipe' and the 'trash of Venice'. He speaks about Cassio as a man who is 'a super slippery knave' and a 'pestilent complete knave' (Act II, scene i).

In contrast with this, Othello's imagery at the beginning of the play conveys the quality of his imagination which is vividly pictorial and often symbolic in emphasis. Thus, in the storm episode, he naturally aligns in imagery the physicality of the storm and the calm that has followed it with his own anxiety and grief at being separated from Desdemona with the joy of his reunification with her. 'If after every tempest come such calms' (Act II, scene i).

Note the way in which he conveys his deepest emotions through the use of natural imagery. Othello seems to find connections between himself and the world in which he lives. He internalises the external world of the elements and of nature, while his recollections of his travels are imaged in exotic terms and the romantic quality of his earlier life:

> Wherein I spake of...
> hair-breadth scapes i' th' imminent deadly breach...
> of antres vast, and deserts idle
> Rough quarries, rocks and hills, whose heads touch
> heaven.   (Act I, scene iii)

Finally, there is the striking imagery of war. The vocabulary of war comes easily to Othello, and in warfare he finds a positive value. Othello's imagery is wide-ranging and sweeping in scope. It is beautifully clear and concrete.

Iago's imagery, by contrast, is limited and functional. It refers to the world of men and things, the world of the material and the routine. Even when Iago reaches for colourful imagery, his words have none of the majesty of those of Othello. When Iago thinks that Othello may have had an affair with Emilia, he says:

> the thought whereof
> doth like a poisonous mineral gnaw my inwards
>
> (Act II, scene i)

It is interesting that Iago uses a simile rather than a metaphor. This indicates one of the differences between his mind and that of Othello. Othello characteristically uses metaphor because he finds it natural to make connections between himself and the world he inhabits, while Iago the cynic insists on his separateness from what he observes. Hence, when he uses imagery, he tends to prefer the more deliberate and considered form of the simile.

Iago's functional approach to language is well depicted in his imagery of the body as gardens and the will as gardener:

> our bodies are gardens, to the which our
> wills are gardeners.
>
> (Act I, scene iii)

Note the reductive nature of his imagery. When Othello greets Desdemona with a profound joy on the safe arrival in Cyprus, having been separated by a violent storm, Iago is quick to puncture this sense of bliss and happiness. In an aside, he says:

> O, y'are well tuned now,
> But I'll set down the pegs that make this music.
>
> (Act II, scene i)

Iago has decided to turn the harmony of the relationship between Othello and Desdemona into dissonance. He will 'turn her virtue into pitch…'

Iago's use of animal imagery is distinctive. Note his use of the imagery of hunting, catching and trapping:

to catch so great a fly as Cassio…
the net that shall enmesh them all.
                    (Act II, scene iii)

These highlight and pinpoint the fact that Iago's mindset operates at a very base level, a level which sees human beings simply as preying on one another in a coarse and vulgar manner.

As the play progresses and Othello becomes infected with Iago's poison, his use of imagery becomes the same as that used by Iago. He begins to use animal imagery suggestive of darkness and confinement in a cistern. In his only soliloquy, which comes halfway through the 'temptation scene' (Act III, scene iii), Othello speaks about his preference to being a 'toad' living 'upon the vapour in a dungeon' than to have a woman who will betray him for other men. Later on he condemns Desdemona using violent images: 'lewd minx' and 'fair devil'. All of this imagery is indicative of how much he has allowed his mind and soul to be polluted by Iago's foul lies and insinuations.

The imagery of Othello's final speech in Act V is particularly affecting. The language used by Othello in this scene echoes the romantic passion and vision that characterised his earlier speeches. He speaks about plucking the rose and how his sorrow is 'heavenly'.

Interestingly, a lot of Othello's utterances are fragmented in this final scene. They serve the function of showing us what he has lost:

of one whose hand
Like the base Judean, threw a pearl away,
Richer than all this tribe…
of one whose subdued eyes…
Drops tears as fast as the Arabian trees.
                    (Act V, scene ii)

These images make clear to us the profound sense of loss and tragic waste that has been experienced by Othello.

ISSUES

Shakespeare's use of imagery also serves to underline and pinpoint certain issues that are important in the context and value system of this tragedy.

Since the play deals primarily with the enigmatic and destructive effects of evildoing and, to a lesser extent, the nature of goodness, certain image patterns emerge. Darkness, deceit, ugliness and hell are used to underline the reality of evil in the play.

Both Iago and Emilia use language that is reductive and highlights their deep sense of disillusionment and cynicism. This is evident when they speak about love, relationships and sex. Iago debases love and sex by reducing them to mere appetite, in his creed love is merely 'lust of the blood and permission of the will' (Act I, scene iii).

His vision of love and its real nature become steadily diminished through his use of reductive imagery. Speaking about Desdemona's love for Othello he comments bitterly:

> her delicate tenderness will find itself abus'd, begin to heave the
> gorge, disrelish and abhor the Moor.
>
> (Act II, scene i)

Later on, this same approach to sexuality is echoed by Emilia. We see the same reductive and disillusioned cynicism in her words when she speaks about relationships between men and women:

> Tis not a year or two shows us a man
> They are but stomachs and we all but food,
> They eat us hungrily and when they are full
> They belch us.
>
> (Act III, scene iv)

Othello finally comes to see Desdemona's sexuality in the same terms as merely lustful. He comments on the ungovernable 'appetites' of the 'delicate creatures men marry and call theirs', and later he refers to the moistness of Desdemona's hand as indicating her wantonness:

> This hand of yours requires
> A sequester from liberty, fasting and prayer…
> For here's a young and sweating devil here,
>
> (Act III, scene iv)

Shakespeare reveals how corruption within a person is revealed through their particular use of language and imagery.

The diabolical references and imagery used within the play are particularly associated with Iago. He compares Othello to the devil. He tells Brabantio: 'The Devil will make a grandsire of you'. His influence over Othello becomes apparent when the latter adopts the same type of language. He begins to speak about his wife as a 'fair devil':

> Heaven truly knows, that thou art false as hell...
> She's like a liar gone to burning hell.
>
> (Act V, scene ii)

At the play's end, Othello sees himself consigned to Hell:

> Whip me you devils
> From the possession of this heavenly sight
> Blow me about in winds
> roast me in sulphur
> Wash me in steep-down gulfs of liquid fire.
>
> (Act V, scene ii)

His sense of repentance is such that he feels he is only worthy of being punished in the fires of hell.

Shakespeare uses a contrasting pattern of images to show goodness. This is revealed through the use of light, beauty and divine images. There are heavenly references used about the nature of Desdemona: 'The divine Desdemona'; 'full of most blessed condition'; 'O she was heavenly true'.

Heavenly references also appear alongside the evildoing in the play: 'Heaven stops the nose at it'; 'O the more angel she and you the blacker devil'; 'No by this heavenly light'; and

> Lest being like one of heaven, the devils themselves
> Should fear to seize thee, therefore be double-damn'd
> Swear thou art honest.
>
> (Act IV, scene ii)

The use of such images serves to present a rich contrast within this play in the presentation of the different themes and issues.

IRONY

Irony involves a discrepancy between what is said, implied or suggested, and what in fact constitutes reality or the truth of things. Iago is the supreme dissembler in the play: a man who appears to be 'honest' and who in reality is little more than a 'demi-devil'. Iago is at the root of nearly all the irony used in this play.

There are different kinds of irony used in this play:

- Dramatic irony
- Situational irony
- Verbal irony

The false perception that Iago embodies honesty in his persona contributes to a good deal of the irony in the play. Every character falls victim to this misconception of Iago.

From the outset of this drama, there are continual references to the fact that Iago is an honest man who is totally trustworthy. Othello repeatedly refers to Iago as an honest man: 'A man he is of honesty and trust'; 'Honest Iago that looks dead with grieving'; 'I know thy honesty and love doth mince this matter'. Cassio uses him as a confidante when he finds himself dismissed from his job and entreats him as 'honest Iago'. All these statements are made against the background of Iago's contriving and devious plotting to actually destroy the people themselves.

Othello is a particularly painful play to watch because of the weight of dramatic irony deployed in the action. A.C. Bradley comments: 'Nowhere else in Shakespeare do we hold our breath in such anxiety and for so long as in the later acts of *Othello*.'

But from the opening of this drama, Shakespeare forces us, the spectators, to become aware of the situations in which we see others in the play innocently enmesh themselves. In the first scene we become privy to Iago's hidden motivations: 'I am not what I am'; 'I hate the Moor'. He announces his plans to destroy Othello's peace of mind 'practising upon his peace and quiet/Even to madness'.

All of these insights contribute a great deal to the splendid dramatic irony that is a fundamental part of this play, and they operate to sustain audience interest and create tension.

The play's action arouses in us a continuous, unrelieved movement between what Bradley calls 'sickening hope and dreadful expectation'. Perhaps this is part of its cathartic effect.

In addition, the play abounds with numerous examples of situational irony. People are placed in situations where they are totally unaware of the fact that their actions and words are operating on another totally different level. For example, when Emilia verbally denounces the fact that some villain has insinuated vile ideas about Desdemona to her husband she rants and raves to her husband telling him that such a 'scurvy fellow' should be whipped naked through the world 'from the east to the west' and that 'hell' should 'gnaw his bones'. Such comments are amusing to a certain extent, given that they are articulated in front of the very villain himself, Iago!

Shakespeare's use of situational irony in this drama is certainly not always comic. In truth, it has a very chilling and potent effect on an audience. This is evident in the story of Desdemona. She is a woman of exceptional virtue, goodness and purity; and yet she is a woman who from early on in the drama becomes a target of foul suspicion on the part of her husband and who even as he kills her can speak about that 'whiter skin of hers than snow'.

Part of the effect of Shakespeare's use of such irony is to highlight the innate blindness within characters to the truth underlying human nature and to the depths of evildoing.

It is a tribute to Shakespeare that he manages to work into his drama a clever mixture of different layers of irony that blend together to create an intriguing story that fascinates and also shocks both reader and audience.

KEY QUOTATIONS AND HOW TO USE THEM

Below is a list of quotations arranged according to theme and character. Study the quotations and think about what they say about a particular character or theme. Pay attention to where in the plot these quotations appear. You can use these quotations to answer exam questions. Remember that almost half the marks are awarded for good use of appropriate quotation.

OTHELLO'S CHARACTER

'I fetch my life and being from men of royal siege…
But that I love the gentle Desdemona.' (Act I, scene ii)

'I must be found.
My parts, my title, and my perfect soul,
Shall manifest me rightly.' (Act I, scene ii)

'Keep up your bright swords, for the dew will
rust 'em.' (Act I, scene ii)

'the valiant Moor' (Act I, scene iii)

'Rude am I in my speech
And little blest with the set phrase of peace…' (Act I, scene iii)

'And little of this great world can I speak
More than pertains to feats of broil and battle.' (Act I ,scene iii)

'She lov'd me for the dangers I had pass'd
And I lov'd her that she did pity them.' (Act I, scene iii)

'Othello, the fortitude of the place…' (Act I, scene iii)

'The Moor a free and open nature too
That thinks men honest that but seem to be so
And will as tenderly be led by the nose…
As asses are.' (Act I, scene iii)

'The Moor, howbeit that I endure him not
Is of a constant, noble, loving nature.' (Act II, scene i)

'I had rather be a toad
And live upon the vapour in a dungeon
Than keep a corner in a thing I love
For others' uses.' (Act III, scene iii)

'The Moor already changes with my poison.' (Iago speaking about Othello, Act III,
scene iii)

'thou hast set me on the rack.' (Act III, scene iii)

'Arise black vengeance from thy hollow cell
Yield up, O love, thy crown, and hearted throne, To tyrannous hate' (Act III, scene iii)

'his unbookish jealousy' (Act IV, scene i)

'Is this the noble Moor, whom our full senate
Call all in all sufficient? This the noble nature
Whom passion could not shake? Whose solid virtue
The shot of accident, nor dart of chance
Could neither graze nor pierce?' (Act IV, scene i)

'O the more angel she
And you the blacker devil!' (Act V, scene ii)

'O thou dull Moor.' (Act V, scene ii)

'Whip me you devils
From the possession of this heavenly sight
Blow me in winds, roast me in sulphur
Wash me in steep-down gulfs of liquid fire.' (Act V, scene ii)

'rash and most unfortunate man' (Act V, scene ii)

'O thou Othello, that wert once so good
Fall'n in the practice of a damn'd slave.' (Act V, scene ii)

'Speak of me as I am…
Of one that lov'd not wisely, but too well
Of one not easily jealous, but being wrought
perplex'd in the extreme, of one whose hand
Like the base Judean threw a pearl away
Richer than all his tribe.' (Act V, scene ii)

IAGO'S CHARACTER

'I follow him to serve my turn upon him…
in following him I follow but myself…
not I for Love and duty
But seeming so for my peculiar end.' (Act I, scene i)

'I am not what I am.' (Act I, scene i)

'though I do hate him as I do hell's pains…' (Act I, scene i)

'love…is merely a lust of the blood, and permission
of the will.' (Act I, scene iii)

'as little a web as this will ensnare as great a fly as Cassio…
I will catch
you in your own courtesies.' (Act II, scene i)

'My boat sails freely, both with wind and stream.' (Act II, scene iii)

'Dull not device by coldness and delay' (Act II, scene iii)

'my wayward husband' (Act II, scene iii)

'O damn'd Iago, O inhuman dog' (Act V, scene i)

'This is the night that makes me or fordoes me quite.' (Act V, scene i)

'a notorious villain' (Act V, scene ii)

'a damned slave' (Act V, scene ii)

'where is this viper?' (Act V, scene ii)

'that demi-devil' (Act V, scene ii)

'Demand me nothing, what you know, you know
From this time forth I never will speak word.' (Act V, scene ii)

'O Spartan dog.' (Act V, scene ii)

'hellish villain' (Act V, scene ii)

DESDEMONA'S CHARACTER

'here's my husband
And so much duty as my mother show'd
To you, preferring you before her father
So much I challenge, that I may profess,
Due to the Moor my lord.' (Act I, scene iii)

'my heart's subdued
Even to the utmost pleasure of my lord.' (Act I, scene iii)

'The divine Desdemona' (Act I, scene iii)

'she is so free, so kind, so apt, so blessed a disposition that
she holds it a vice in her goodness not to do more than
she is requested.
The virtuous Desdemona.' (Act I, scene iii)

'she is fram'd as fruitful
As the free elements…
His soul is so infetter'd to her love
That she may make, unmake do what she list
With his weak function.' (Act II, scene iii)

'My lord is not my lord.' (Act II, scene iv)

'Something sure of state…
Hath puddled his clear spirit.' (Act III, scene iv)

'we must think men are not gods.' (Act III, scene iv)

'Alas, what ignorant sin have I committed?' (Act IV, scene ii)

'By heaven, you do me wrong.' (Act IV, scene ii)

'his unkindness may defeat my life
But never taint my love.' (Act IV, scene ii)

'whiter skin of hers than snow
And smooth as monumental alabaster…
yet she must die else
she'll betray more men. (Act V, scene ii)

'Heaven
Have mercy on me.' (Act V, scene ii)

'never lov'd Cassio
But with such general warranty of heaven

As I might love.' (Act V, scene ii)

'a guiltless death I die.' (Act V, scene ii)

'she was chaste, she lov'd thee cruel Moor.' (Act V, scene ii)

CASSIO'S CHARACTER

'Michael Cassio, a Florentine' (Act I, scene i)

'Cassio's a proper man…
He has a person and a smooth dispose
To be suspected, fram'd to make women false.' (Act I, scene iii)

'he is rash, and very sudden in choler.
Iago speaking about Michael Cassio.' (Act II, scene I).

'Reputation, reputation, reputation…
I have lost the immortal part of
myself, and what remains is bestial.' (Act II, scene iii)

'Cassio rules in Cyprus' (Act V, scene ii)

JEALOUSY

'I put the Moor
At least, into a jealousy so strong
That judgement cannot cure.' (Act II, scene i)

'beware my lord of jealousy
It is the green-eyed monster, which doth mock
That meat it feeds on.' (Act III, scene iii)

'trifles light as air
Are to the jealous, confirmations strong
As proofs of Holy Writ.' (Act III, scene iii)

'my noble Moor
Is true of mind, and made of no such baseness
As jealous creatures are.' (Act III, scene iv)

'It is a monster
begot upon itself, born on itself.' (Act III, scene iv)

'if Cassio do remain
He has a daily beauty in his life
That makes me ugly.' (Act V, scene i)

EVIL

'Hell and night
Must bring this monstrous birth to the world's light.' (Act I, scene iii)

'practising upon his peace and quiet
Even to madness…' (Act II, scene i)

'Knavery's plain face is never seen, till us'd.' (Act II, scene i)

'Divinity of hell
When devils will their blackest sins put on
That do suggest at first with heavenly shows
As I do now.' (Act II, scene iii)

'Damn her lewd minx: O damn her…
furnish me with some swift means of death
For the fair devil.' (Act III, scene iii)

GOODNESS

'So will I turn her virtue into pitch
And out of her own goodness make the net
That shall enmesh 'em all.' (Act II, scene iii)

'This deed of thine is no more worthy heaven
Than thou wast worthy her.' (Act V, scene ii)

DECEPTION

'In following him, I follow but myself...
I am not what I am.' (Act I, scene i)

'Yet for necessity of present life
I must show out a flag, and sign of love
Which is indeed but sign.' (Act I, scene i)

'Thus do I make my fool my purse' (Act I, scene iii)

'Divinity of hell
When devils will their blackest sins put on
They do suggest at first with heavenly shows
As I do now.' (Act II, scene iii)

'An honest man he is, and hates the slime
That sticks on filthy deeds.' (Act V, scene ii)

RACIAL PREJUDICE

'an old black ram
Is tupping your white ewe' (Act I, scene i)

'a frail vow, betwixt an erring barbarian
and a super-subtle Venetian.' (Act I, scene iii)

'black Othello' (Act II, scene iii)

IRONY

'By Janus I think no.'
(Act I, scene ii: Iago swears an oath to the God of light and truth.)

'A man he is of honesty and trust.'
(Act I, scene iii: Othello speaks about Iago.)

'My life upon her faith: honest Iago.'
(Act I, scene iii: Othello speaks to Iago. This is a particularly ironic statement, since Othello does indeed give his life at the end of the play when he recognises that Desdemona was a woman of fidelity and honour.)

'For I have lost him on a dangerous sea.'
(Act II, scene i: Cassio speaks about Othello.)

'Honest Iago, that looks dead with grieving
Speak who began this?' (Act II, scene iii)

'I know Iago
They honesty and love doth mince this matter
Making it light to Cassio.' (Act II, scene iii)

'I never knew
A Florentine more kind and honest.'
(Act III, scene i: Cassio speaks about Iago.)

'For thy solicitor shall rather die
Than give thy cause away.'
(Act III, scene iii: Desdemona speaks to Cassio about the fact that she would rather die than give up on his cause.)

'This fellow's of exceeding honesty
And knows all qualities, with a learned spirit
Of human dealing.'
(Act III, scene iii: Othello speaks about Iago.)

'I have moved my lord in his behalf and hope all will be well.'
(Act III, scene iv: Desdemona speaks to a clown about Cassio.)

'The Moor's abus'd by some outrageous knave
Some base notorious knave, some scurvy fellow.'
(Act IV, scene ii: Emilia speaks to her husband Iago.)

'O brave Iago, honest and just
That hast such noble sense of thy friend's wrong.' (Act V, scene i)

Stage directions: Enter Iago with a light. (Act V, scene i)

'An honest man he is, and hates the slime
That sticks on filthy deeds.'
(Act V, scene ii: Othello speakes to Emilia about Iago.)

SUMMARY OF SOLILOQUIES AND ASIDES

S tudy the Soliloquy in Shakespeare's Tragedies (p.4). Remember that Shakespeare makes use of the soliloquy to give the audience a deeper insight into a character than we might gain from their conversations with different people. A soliloquy is a speech expressed by a character aloud while he/she stands alone on the stage.

In *Othello*, Iago is the pivotal character around which all the events and the plot revolve. He turns out to be the main protagonist who uses the soliloquy to frame his plot and assess the other characters around him.

Shakespeare gives this villain several soliloquies and asides, all of which enable the audience to see how powerful a figure he is in the context of this tragic drama.

Othello has just two soliloquies in the entire play.

For each soliloquy and aside, consider the following points:

- Where in the play does this soliloquy/aside occur?
- What do we learn about the person from the soliloquy/aside?
- What images are used and what function do they serve?
- What does this soliloquy/aside tell us about the action/plot?
- Are there certain themes expressed in the soliloquy/aside?

IAGO
Soliloquy 1: Act I, scene iii, lines 381–402

This occurs at the conclusion of the first Act of the play. Iago cynically assesses the defects of Roderigo and Othello. Iago is using Roderigo merely for his money, he calls him a 'snipe'. Iago also says that he hates the Moor and decides to use the flimsy idea that he is committing adultery with Emilia as an excuse to avenge himself. Cassio will be the scapegoat used by Iago to further his plot, since Cassio is handsome and popular with women. We learn that Othello is gullible: he is like an 'ass' and is unable to see through people. Images of hell and night suggest that Iago is aware of the diabolic nature of his plot but he is determined to go ahead with it.

Aside 1: Act II, scene i, lines 167–77

Cassio has been showing a good deal of courtesy to the two ladies, Desdemona and Emilia, on their arrival in Cyprus. Cassio pays particular attention to Desdemona. Iago watches all of this behaviour and decides to use these gestures to destroy the two people, Cassio and Desdemona, claiming that 'as little a web as this will ensnare as great a fly as Cassio'. Iago's power and wicked intentions are evident here.

Soliloquy 2: Act II, scene i, lines 211–37

All the main characters have arrived in Cyprus and Iago fabricates his plot here in more detail. Iago uses the idea of Othello's supposed adultery with Emilia as an excuse for his revenge. He plans to arouse jealousy in the soul of Othello about an adulterous relationship between Desdemona and Michael Cassio. He will use Roderigo as a pawn to provoke a fight with Cassio under the false assumption that he can further his cause with Desdemona. The images used here show us Iago's deep-seated malice and destructive cynicism: 'an ass', 'poor trash of Venice' and 'knavery's plain face'.

Soliloquy 3: Act II, scene iii, lines 44–58

Iago is planning to get Michael Cassio drunk. Iago has managed to get Roderigo and the guards on duty drunk while he remains sober and engineers his plot. Iago uses vivid imagery to describe his vicious plot: 'My boat sails freely, both with wind and stream.' This type of language suits his purposes, as it cloaks his real intentions.

Soliloquy 4: Act II, scene iii, lines 327–53

In this soliloquy, Iago justifies his evil intrigues and schemes so far in the drama. Iago has managed to dishonour Cassio and get him dismissed from his position as lieutenant. He has counselled Cassio to intercede with Desdemona in order to reinstate himself in the army. Iago announces that he will use Desdemona's virtues against her to destroy everyone: her virtues will be like a net that will enmesh them all. The images used show an awareness by Iago that he is committing evil: 'Divinity of hell/When devils will their blackest sins put on...As I do now.'

Aside 2: Act II, scene iii, lines 373–8

Iago explains that he will develop his plot in two ways: he will get his wife, Emilia, a position working close to Desdemona, and he will organise a situation where Othello will find Cassio and Desdemona together.

Soliloquy 5: Act iii, scene iii, lines 326–38

This soliloquy occurs in the middle of the 'temptation scene'. Emilia has just handed a handkerchief to Iago which she found on the ground and which belongs to Desdemona. Iago decides to plant this handkerchief in Cassio's apartment. Iago announces that Othello is already beginning to change with 'my poison'. He states that Othello's peace of mind is gone forever.

Aside 3: Act IV, scene i, lines 93–7

Iago announces that he will deceive Othello even more by questioning Cassio about his relationship with Desdemona. In reality he will ask him about Bianca, the 'strumpet'.

Soliloquy 6: Act V, scene i, lines 11–22

Iago plans to kill Roderigo and have Cassio murdered because he fears exposure. Iago's jealousy is dominant: he claims that Cassio has 'a daily beauty in his life/That makes me ugly.' The images used by Iago in this soliloquy include the disease image of 'quat' to describe the irritating presence of Roderigo in his life.

OTHELLO

Othello has only two soliloquies. One occurs in the middle of the 'temptation scene'. The second one occurs in the final scene as he is about to kill his wife in what he sees is an action of justice.

Soliloquy 1: Act III, scene iii, lines 262–83

Iago's poison about Desdemona's supposed adulterous affair has eroded Othello's confidence in himself. Othello is still convinced of the absolute honesty of Iago. He feels insecure about his status as a Moor ('Haply, for I am black') and his age also bothers him ('for I am declin'd/Into the vale of years'). Othello's use of imagery in this soliloquy highlights the subtle but real deterioration in his soul: 'I had rather be a toad/And live upon the vapour in a dungeon.'

Soliloquy 2: Act V, scene ii, lines 1–22

This soliloquy occurs in the final scene, as Othello makes his way to the bedroom to kill his wife, under the illusion that he is acting as an agent of divine justice. The soliloquy is rich with irony. Othello is armed with a light and speaks about putting out the light, not realising that it is Iago who has blotted out the light of his faith in the truth about his wife.

The images used in this soliloquy are positive and filled with beauty: 'pluck the rose'; 'whiter skin of hers than snow'; 'chaste stars'. These images turn out to be dramatically ironic as Othello has been deceived about his wife's fidelity.

HOW TO STUDY *OTHELLO*

THE COMPARATIVE QUESTION

Under the Comparative section of the exam, you will be required to compare *Othello* with two other texts under certain modes. The modes for the Comparative question are:

- Literary genre
- Cultural context
- General vision and viewpoint
- Themes/Issues

Literary Genre

The genre of a text means the type of text that it is: a play, a film or a narrative (e.g. novel, memoir, biography or autobiography). In the case of *Othello*, the literary genre is that of a **tragic play**, which is written in five Acts.

    Othello is a tragedy about incomprehension. The tragic experience is concerned with a loss of faith. Othello, who is a Moor and a cultural outsider, allows himself to be deceived into believing his wife has been unfaithful.

    His tragedy is rooted in his inexperience of Venetian culture, together with a misplaced and unqualified trust in the honesty and loyalty of Iago, his ensign. He accepts Iago's insinuations as truth, and acts on them without thinking. In the end, he trusts the word of Iago so much that he even murders his own wife. Only after the murder the full truth about Iago's wickedness becomes exposed – and Othello then kills himself.

    In an assessment of the genre of Othello, the following questions must be asked:

- How is the story constructed? What is the structure of the play?
- How does Shakespeare use the soliloquy to assist in the construction of the tragedy?
- What are the meanings of the recurring images, metaphors and symbols? What is their function in the tragedy?
- What is the function of irony in the tragedy?
- What scenes contribute the most to the tragedy?
- Is there a sub plot? If so, how does it relate to the main plot?
- How does the playwright make use of character, colour and contrast to tell the story?

STRUCTURE

The play is structured into five different **Acts**. In each Act, the plot is developed further. Iago is the character who controls the action and, therefore, he speaks in soliloquies or asides which show his dominance in the play.

Act III scene iii is the **turning point** in the tragedy. At this stage, a change has come over Othello. Iago's poisonous insinuations have deeply affected Othello. Othello plans to murder his wife and orders Iago to kill Cassio.

The **time sequence** of the play is short. The entire action takes place over a period of four or five days. Act I opens on Othello's wedding night. That same night he is dispatched to Cyprus. Act II opens with the arrival of all the main characters, including Othello, in Cyprus three days later. The night after the arrival in Cyprus, Cassio is dismissed from his post as general. Act III begins the day after Cassio's dismissal. That same day, the 'temptation scene' (Act III, scene iii) occurs. Here, in the garden, Iago poisons Othello's mind about his wife's infidelity. That same day, the handkerchief is lost by Desdemona and later found by Emilia. She gives it to Iago and he plants it in Cassio's chamber almost immediately. Cassio's death is organised to be carried out within the next three days. Othello himself undertakes to kill Desdemona. Act IV takes place with Othello's return to Venice. Othello humiliates Desdemona publicly by striking her and later on treating her as a 'strumpet'. This Act concludes with the conversation between Emilia and Desdemona about marital infidelity.

Act V is full of action. The last scene of this Act dramatises the death of the leading protagonists and the exposure of the villainous machinations of Iago.

IMAGERY

Study the chapter on Language and Imagery (p.53), which will give you more points that can be used in an answer on literary genre.

Much of the imagery in the play highlights the predominant themes and issues. There are certain recurring images, e.g. light and darkness, disease and poison. The images of **light and darkness** include images of heaven and hell, black and white, angels and devils, etc. The images of **disease and poison** are used to show the corrupting effects of Iago's intrigues.

Symbols and images of **repulsive animals and grotesque behaviour** are also used frequently both by Iago and later on by Othello, once he has allowed himself to become corrupted into believing his wife is unfaithful. Several of the scenes in the play take place at night, showing the dominance of evil in the action.

Cultural context

The cultural context means the particular type of **social background** and influences that underlie the society that is represented in the text. The cultural backdrop of *Othello* depicts the worlds of Venice and Cyprus. In both of these places, there is a specific value system. Venice is a rich and powerful place, where the value system rests firmly on power, money, material comfort and male control. The societies in both Venice and Cyprus are **male-dominated** and women are clearly subordinate and second-class citizens. Women themselves are not just treated with contempt and disdain but certain qualities such as loyalty, fidelity and purity are not expected of the woman. They are largely seen as puppets or pawns and in many instances they operate as whores who exist to satisfy the male. Women in this culture are trivialised, the bonds of marriage and relationships are belittled and treated with derision and disrespect.

The surface of Venetian society is sophisticated and elegant. This is mere appearance only: we learn from several comments in the play that it is a society where marital betrayal is the norm and where men can have several different liaisons, including those with prostitutes.

Othello belongs to the culture of North Africa, since he is a Moor. He is, therefore, an outsider in this society.

Part of the cultural context of this play is the existence of the **Venetian senate**. The senate in Venice embodies order, reason, justice and balance. Ancient laws and established customs control violence and ensure the safety and wellbeing of the individual and society. Brabantio's grievances are examined here in a court of law. They are judged by reason and the verdict is enforced by civic power.

The senate is also the place where the actions of the Turks are examined and their true purpose is penetrated. The senate makes sense of the frantic and contradictory messages that pour in from the fleet, and the necessary defence is arranged.

In this culture, self-control is desirable. It is a trait that is especially valuable in soldiers. Othello is a good soldier and a man who is seen to possess a high degree of self-control. His lineage is as royal and as wealthy as any Venetian, so the senate see him as 'the valiant Moor'.

The two lovers, Desdemona and Othello, are surrounded by the governors of Venice who control passions and enforce law and reason. Here, in this context, they are forced to explain how they fell in love and to justify this love for each other.

The cultural framework that underpins this society has very clear customs, traditions and modes of operation. The boundaries between men and women are clearly defined.

General vision and viewpoint

'General vision and viewpoint' can be defined as the author/playwright/director's vision of life and human nature as depicted in the text. It incorporates the **storyline**, **themes** and **characters** represented.

The general vision and viewpoint of this play is that the people involved in the action are unwittingly caught in a situation (or net) from which there is **no escape**. The power of **evil** to deceive and wreak havoc is another chilling aspect of the general vision and viewpoint in this tragedy.

The play concludes with the death of the tragic hero and the restoration of harmony in society. Iago is captured and it is presumed that he will be punished for his crimes. The general impression left to us is that his evil is of an ambiguous nature, the motivations underlying his actions are deliberately left obscure.

Another aspect of the general vision and viewpoint comes at the conclusion of this play. Here we see how evil is punished, but not before it has done a great deal of **harm** in the play. The **power of the woman** to change and grow in moral stature and to reveal the underlying corruption within this society can be seen in Emilia's attack on Othello and her corresponding defence of Desdemona. Emilia plays a large part in the vindication of Desdemona's virtue and honour. It is she who heroically defends Desdemona's purity and goodness, and steadfastly confirms her innocence. She dies in this act of bravery and courage.

Othello's repentance, together with the execution of judgement on himself, is an affirmation of his desire to remain loyal to Venice.

In the general vision and viewpoint of Othello, there is a sense that in some ways evil is punished and good finally triumphs, even if it survives at an enormous price, i.e. the loss of human life.

Themes/Issues

The play deals with a number of different themes and issues:

- Dissimulation
- Jealousy
- Racial prejudice
- Women
- Reputation
- Justice

See pages 39–52 for further exploration of these themes and issues.

Key situations

In studying the play for the Comparative section of the exam, it is useful to be able to identify two or three **key situations** and use them for the different modes that you are writing on.

Here are some examples of key situations in Othello.

Act I, scene i: The opening scene provides a lot of context for the audience.

Act III, scene iii: This is the 'temptation scene'.

Act III, scene iii: The loss of the handkerchief.

Act V, scene ii: The concluding scene and the exposure of Iago.

Checklists

When you are writing on any of the different modes for the Comparative section, it can help if you have checklists to hand. Try using some of the checklists below. They will help you to construct answers on any of the Comparative questions that may come up in the exam.

CHECKLIST FOR LITERARY GENRE

- How is the story told: narrative, dialogue, soliloquy or verse?
- Why is the story told in this way?
- Is there one plot or are there subplots? Do these relate? If so, how? Why?
- What are the tensions in the plot?
- Identify the conflict, climax, falling action and resolution in the text.
- Is the text a comedy, tragedy, melodrama, satire, thriller or romance?
- Are there repeated symbols and/or colours in the text? How and why are they used?
- How are the different characters drawn by the author?

CHECKLIST FOR THEMES/ISSUES

- What are the main themes/issues in the text?
- How are these themes/issues shown?
- How does the storyline broaden our understanding of a particular theme/issue?
- What are the key situations that illustrate the themes/issues most clearly?
- What statements are made in the text about the relevant themes/issues?
- Were the themes/issues treated in a positive or negative way?
- Did the themes/issues change at any stage? Where and how did the change occur?
- What viewpoints did the themes/issues offer to the reader?
- How was the interest of the reader/audience maintained in relation to the themes/issues?

CHECKLIST FOR CULTURAL CONTEXT

- What is the social or class background?
- In what time/era is the text set?
- What are the roles of men and women?
- Is work important in the lives of the people who inhabit the text?
- What type of value system is represented?
- What values are important in the text (honour, loyalty, courage, virtue, power, etc.)?
- What are the dominant power structures?
- What are the social customs, traditions and rituals?
- Is marriage important in this society?
- Does education play a role in the society?
- What is the philosophy of life of the main character?

CHECKLIST FOR GENERAL VISION AND VIEWPOINT

- What exactly is the author saying about life?
- Is the overall vision and viewpoint consistent throughout or does it change?
- Is the vision and viewpoint positive or negative?
- What do you learn about life from the vision and viewpoint?
- What key situations reveal the general vision and viewpoint? How is this done?

THE SINGLE TEXT QUESTION

At Higher Level English it is important to be able to analyse the **type** of text you are working with (e.g. play or novel) and to understand fully the motivations of the various **characters** presented at every stage in the plot.

Othello is a Shakespearean tragedy. In order to answer Single Text questions, it is important to understand what exactly a Shakespearean tragedy is. Try to note the particular aspects in the play that make it tragic. Form your own opinions on the main hero or protagonist. You must have an understanding of the **tragic flaw** in Othello's character and you must be able to identify this throughout the play, pinpointing certain key events and quotations.

It is vital to have a clear understanding of the **plot**. Sometimes it is useful to draw a map showing all of the actions in the play and all of the consequences for these actions.

Once you have come to an understanding of the plot and of what contributes to the main action in the play, begin to study the main **characters**. The characters give rise to the action in the play's plot, and also to the main issues or themes that are dealt with in the play.

In this play, in your analysis of character, and especially that of the main protagonists, it can help to understand the character in the light of what other people say about him/

her. Also, in Shakespearean drama, we can learn a lot about character through analysing the asides or the **soliloquies** expressed by a character. Shakespeare manages to give the villainous Iago many asides and soliloquies in *Othello*. Through these, we gain an insight into his frame of mind and what is motivating him in thought and in action.

Certain **images** can give us a new insight into a character. Images can help us towards painting a picture of a person and what it is that motivates their actions. Take, for example, Othello's claim that he has reached the peak of happiness in his relationship with Desdemona: 'If I were now to die/'Twere now to be most happy.' This image is a powerful statement that he has reached the pinnacle of happiness in his marriage to Desdemona. Equally, Desdemona's quiet but sincere statement before the Venetian signory that 'my heart's subdued /Even to the utmost pleasure of my lord' tells us that her commitment to her husband is true and authentic and that her whole life revolves around her husband. These are just some of the many images in *Othello* that reveal the traits of the characters to the audience.

It can help to write out a list of images that are used about a character and to use them for your answers. Try to form your own judgements about the different characters and their behaviour in the play. While study notes can help, it is your own **personal analysis** and **judgements** about the character and what motivates them that are most valuable when it comes to gaining higher marks in the exam!

Once you have an indepth understanding of the characters, begin to look at the main ideas/themes that are expressed in the text. Form your own opinions about these ideas and link them in to the motivations that govern the behaviour of the different people in the play. Many times, imagery and language will reveal to you the main ideas of the text.

It is not enough to extract the central themes/issues of the play: you must go further and see what **statement is being made about these issues/themes**. Take some important scenes and study them individually in more detail. Examine the dramatic function of each scene in the overall structure of the play. Ask the following questions:

*   How does this scene contribute to the subsequent action in the play?
*   Does this scene highlight any new aspects of characters through asides or soliloquies?
*   Has this scene made a statement (or statements) on themes/issues? If so, what is this statement?

Write out your own list of quotations and learn them off. It is vital to be familiar with quotations so that you can weave them in naturally and fluidly to your answers. Practise writing answers to previous exam questions. Try to get to the stage where you are writing your answer in the same time that you will have in your exam, approximately 50 minutes.

HOW TO ANSWER EXAM-STYLE QUESTIONS

One of the easiest mistakes to make when answering exam questions on any area in literature, and especially on Shakespeare's plays, is to tell the story of the plot. Questions at Higher Level English presuppose that you have an intimate knowledge of the text, so it is not necessary to recount exactly what happens at every stage. Exams test your ability to extract certain information and to evaluate it in the light of a question. The Higher Level question also tests your ability to form your own judgements about issues and character motivation. Knowing what information to discard can often be as important as knowing what points to make and what quotations to use.

When answering exam-style questions on the Shakespearean play it is important to look very closely at every word in the question and at the way the question is phrased. Take, for example, a question such as 'Discuss the dramatic significance of Emilia's role in the play *Othello*.' This question is not asking you to write about the character of Emilia; it is asking about her role in the dramatic structure or the plot of the play. If you answer a question like this you need to think about Emillia's function, what part she plays in the plot, and the significance of her role. Simply jotting down all your notes and quotations about Emilia will not be enough to gain that A grade. Spend some time thinking about what she does in the play, and why, and what is the outcome of her action or inaction.

Thinking of a quotation or quotations that have some relation to the question can be a helpful way of getting started on a question. You can then build arguments based on these quotations.

Before you introduce a quotation use a comma and then put inverted commas around the quote, for example, 'Fair is foul and foul is fair.' If the quotation is a full sentence the full stop goes inside the closing inverted comma.

Your answer should be about three or four pages in length. Remember to structure your answer into paragraphs. These can vary in length. Make sure that each paragraph is advancing your argument and is making some point about your answer to the question.

Before constructing any paragraph ask yourself:

- What relation has this paragraph to the question asked?
- How is this paragraph linked with the preceding paragraph?
- What quotation can I use to support the point made in the paragraph?

Avoid the tendency to leave your answer in mid-argument or mid-air. Bring your answer to a logical conclusion and round it off by writing a short but clear **conclusion**.

Your conclusion does not have to be long, but remember, it is the last impression left on your examiner, so make it a good one. You can restate the main points you made during your answer, and you could refer again to the question, showing your stance on it. If you conclude on a quotation, remember: you must have commented on its significance.

SOME COMMON FAULTS

1. Answer is too short.
2. The points mentioned in the question are not addressed.
3. Essay is merely a summary of the play.
4. No suitable quotations or references to the play are used to support the answer.
5. Part or all of the answer is irrelevant.
6. Answer contains padding to make it look longer. This will be penalised.
7. Answer is poorly structured and lacks organisation.
8. Ideas are badly expressed.
9. Answer reveals poor knowledge of or erroneous information about the play.
10. Students answer both alternatives. This is a waste of precious time, as only one alternative counts towards the final mark.

TIPS AND HINTS

1. Know the play thoroughly and be able to quote at will.
2. Read the question carefully more than once.
3. Underline the key words in the question.
4. Ensure that you answer all parts of the question.
5. Write in paragraphs. State your point, develop it and support it with quotations and/ or reference to the play.
6. Write at least three pages.
7. Be careful not to stray from the question into irrelevance.
8. Avoid waffle or padding. This will not fool the experienced examiners who mark your papers.
9. You have 50 minutes to write your answer. Do not exceed this time.
10. Understand clearly the way the characters change as the plot develops.

LEAVING CERTIFICATE ENGLISH: CRITERIA FOR ASSESSMENT

- *Clarity of Purpose:* engagement with the set task (e.g. relevance, focus, originality, freshness, clear aim, understanding of genre).
- *Coherence of Delivery:* ability to sustain the response over the entire answer. Where appropriate this includes continuity of argument, sequencing, management of ideas, choice of reference, use of examples, engagement with texts, control of register and shape, creative modelling.
- *Efficiency of Language Use:* management and control of language to achieve clear communication (e.g. vocabulary, syntax, sentence patterns, paragraph structure, punctuation appropriate to the register, use of lively interesting phrasing, energy, style, fluency appropriate to the task).
- *Accuracy of Mechanics:* spelling, grammar (e.g. appropriate levels of accuracy in spelling, grammatical patterns appropriate to the register).

The marking scheme is:
- Purpose: 18 marks
- Coherence: 18 marks
- Language: 18 marks
- Mechanics: 6 marks

Be sure to keep the criteria for assessment in mind when you are answering exam-style questions.

SAMPLE QUESTIONS AND ANSWERS

The following questions are taken from past Leaving Cert exam papers. In order to gain the maximum benefit from the sample answers, attempt the question yourself first and see how you would structure your answer and what ideas you would use. Then compare your answer with the sample here and see what aspects you might have missed.

Each answer is marked, according to the Leaving Cert guide, under P (purpose), C (coherence), L (language) and M (mechanics).

You could also try reading the answers and marking them yourself, and maybe writing some commentary on how well the question has been answered.

QUESTIONS

'Othello's foolishness and not Iago's cleverness leads to the tragedy in the play.'
Would you agree with this statement about the play? Support your answer with quotation and reference to the play. (2008)

ANSWER

It is not possible to use either the foolishness of Othello nor the cleverness of Iago as an index by which to judge the tragic outcome of this play. It is rather the culmination of different features within these two men that contributes to the tragic outcome. In many ways, it becomes clear that Othello is responsible for his own downfall as his nature is essentially flawed and this leads to some crucially misguided judgements in the play. It is also equally clear that if it were not for Iago's expert knowledge of the vulnerabilities of people, combined with an exceptional degree of malignancy in his nature, the tragedy in this play could have been averted, and Othello would not have found himself reduced to such a tragic state at the end of this play. So, therefore, it is not just foolishness on Othello's part or extreme cleverness on the part of Iago that causes this tragedy.

What contributes to the tragedy that occurs in this play is due in part to particular features in both men, the fact that Iago is a particularly single-minded and evil villain gifted with huge powers, and with a disturbing love of evil for its own sake, and that Othello's experience is limited to the battle ground and he has no knowledge of Venetian society or how human beings interact. In order to understand fully how such a situation occurred within this play it is necessary to examine these aspects of character within both men which ultimately led to the downfall of the tragic hero.

At the beginning of the play, Othello possesses the noble and vital qualities of a tragic hero. He exerts supreme self-control and dignity when confronted with some vile accusations from the enraged Brabantio. Instead of reacting to his hideous insults, 'to fall in love with what she fear'd to look on/It is a judgement maim'd, most imperfect', Othello remains calm and instructs his men to 'put up your bright swords', claiming that my 'parts, my title and my perfect soul/Shall manifest me rightly.' This initial view of Othello is very positive. He seems to be a man who is secure and confident, fully aware of his contribution to the state, and conscious of his royal lineage: 'I fetch my life and being/From men of royal siege.'

However, shortly into the play, we witness the clear disintegration of this man who seems to embody full moral integrity and a clear sense of self-control. A brawl occurs in Cyprus while the army are celebrating the defeat of the Turkish army. When Othello tries to ascertain the detail about this brawl he loses his temper and becomes enraged very quickly. Passion overwhelms him. 'My blood begins my safer guides to rule,' he shouts in an attempt to find out who actually started this brawl. Othello loses his self-control and swiftly dismisses Cassio from his position as lieutenant without any real proof or moral certainty. It is clear that Othello has the mentality of a soldier 'to be once in doubt is once to be resolved', and this flaw of impatience and rashness becomes a defining factor in bringing about the tragic outcome. These are clear character defects in Othello's nature and not just mere foolishness.

Of course, such a flaw would not be fatal without the operations of a sinister villain such as Iago. Labelled as one of Shakespeare's most diabolic and evil characters, Iago possesses the ability to exploit fully the defects and weaknesses of other people. Such is the case with Othello. Iago shrewdly assesses from this small incident that Othello is impatient and rash in action and so he begins to work on his mind eroding his security and peace by means of negative insinuations and implications. He does it in a gradual but very devious and sly manner. Iago exploits the weaknesses of Cassio – a close friend and professional ally of Othello – to lure him into a web of deception so that even from 'as little a web as this' he will 'ensnare a fly as great as Cassio'. Therefore we can see that the tragic action is developed in this play on account of certain patterns of behaviour in both Iago and Othello. Iago's cleverness does indeed enable him to use every opportunity to further his villainous plot while Othello's essential simplicity and inexperience rather than his foolishness aids in his downfall.

Othello's mind is simple and uncomplicated. He is unable to see beyond appearances to the underlying reality. He is utterly convinced of Iago's honesty resting continually on the fact that he is a 'man of honesty and trust'. He underestimates Iago's intelligence and depth of malignancy claiming that 'you may relish him more in the scholar than in the soldier'. These clearly misguided views give Iago a huge power in the play. Othello becomes a victim of false appearances, because of a basic inexperience of life – most of his time has been spent on the battlefield and not in socialising with people. It is this inability to understand character and the capacity for evildoing within the human being that speeds up Iago's plot and generates the tragedy.

It is in the 'temptation scene' in Act III, scene iii that Iago manages to take full advantage of Othello's insecure state of mind. There is no doubt that Iago is supremely clever. He manages skilfully to 'pour' his 'pestilence' into the ear of Othello and twist his mind against his beloved wife. Here in a series of different tactics Iago plays on Othello's vulnerabilities. Othello is an outsider to Venetian culture, a man unacquainted with those 'soft parts of conversation/That chamberers have'. Furthermore, he is 'declin'd/Into the vale of years'. Iago insidiously plays on this self-doubt and in doing so makes his victim lose all sense of reason. Simple insinuations such as 'Ha! I like not that' and the use of animal imagery such as 'goats and monkeys' quickly distorts Othello's mind so that he cannot see anything beyond his own passionate rage and anger. It becomes clear in the 'temptation scene' that both men operate in different ways: one as a tempter providing prompts and cues and the other as the tempted acting on the vile insinuations without any rational thought or self-control. Othello's nature is rash and hot-tempered, while Iago's is skilful and manipulative. So again it is evident that a certain combination of deep-seated villainy and evil together with an acute intelligence in Iago operates on the more weak and vulnerable Othello in order to make him a victim of lies and intrigue.

As the plot unfolds, Othello becomes even more irrational at the thought of his loss of reputation. His pride and egoism become a part of his 'Achilles heel' since he cannot bear the fact that he would be cuckolded by his wife and made a mockery of in front of everyone. Thoughts of Brabantio's earlier warning ('Look to her Moor, if thou hast eyes to see:/She has deceived her father, and may thee') now start to assault his consciousness and he begins to engage in a process of interior doubt and suspicions about his wife. This state leads him to lose that enormous self-control which was a hallmark of his behaviour in the opening scenes. He humiliates Desdemona publicly by striking her in the face. He calls her a devil ('O devil, devil') and a woman of 'well painted passion!' Under the insidious effect of Iago's persistent insinuations about Desdemona's infidelity Othello's mind begins to disintegrate. He descends almost to the level of a beast and this becomes evident from his language patterns and behaviour. In a symbolic act of unity with Iago, he announces: 'I'll tear her all to pieces.' This degeneration of a man who was noble and heroic to a state of irrationality and near savagery leads to his tragedy at the conclusion. It is certainly evident that a good deal of Othello's downfall in the play occurs because Iago manages so successfully to exploit certain basic weaknesses in his character, rather than the fact that Othello is merely foolish.

Iago's single-minded malignancy of nature and expert opportunism all work towards causing the final catastrophe at the end of the play. He uses the conversation between Bianca and Cassio to convince the highly-wrought Othello that they are speaking about Desdemona's infidelity. He also manages through luck and chance to secure evidence in the form of the hanky which he presents to Othello as 'ocular proof'. Through coincidence, fate and misadventure, together with the ability to use situations fortuitously, Iago ensures that Othello becomes convinced enough to decide to murder his wife lest 'she betray more men'.

It seems that by the end of the play the tragedy is inevitable because of the particular nature of both men and their interaction in the play. Iago, an undoubted Machiavellian in his approach to life and a 'demi-devil', is truly one of Shakespeare's most evil characters. Through his sustained crafty wiliness and exceptionally shrewd character, he manages to exploit to full advantage the weakness of every character in the play, and in particular that of Othello the tragic hero. Othello, the noble Moor and valiant general of Venice, freely allows himself to lose faith in his own wife and to believe the vile lies and suggestions that Iago whispers in his ear.

Tragedy dictates that it must ultimately be the flawed nature of the tragic hero which causes his downfall. Shakespeare restores Othello's dignity at the end of the play, as Othello kills himself in an act of repentance and what he believes is justice.

It becomes clear that from the outset of this play the tragic action that culminates in the deaths of the main protagonists is rooted in a combination of what Coleridge described as a 'motiveless malignancy' and a particularly perverse individual in the figure of the villain Iago. This, of course, is combined with the fact that Othello is an alien in the Venetian culture, a man whose experience of life is limited and whose judgements are made on face value. It is the combination and operations between both men which contribute to the tragic action in this play, and not just merely foolishness on the part of Othello and cleverness within Iago.

P: 18/18
C: 18/18
L: 18/18
M: 6/6
Total: 60/60

COMMENT

This is an excellent answer that deserves full marks. The answer takes a clear stance early on with regard to the question and sustains the response right through to the end in a balanced manner. The answer makes very good use of appropriate and relevant quotation to support all points made. At every stage in the answer the purpose is maintained, i.e. the question is answered and this response is skilfully carried right through each paragraph. In other words, expert coherence is established in the response. The language used is original and fresh and the writer shows an indepth knowledge of this play.

QUESTIONS

'What impact does the theme or issue of Appearance and Reality have on the play *Othello*? In your answer use quotation from or reference to the play.'

ANSWER

Shakespeare manages to construct a powerful drama where appearances belie the underlying truth at every stage in this play's operations. This is because both character and action are not what they appear to be. Perhaps the root of this discrepancy lies in the figure of that most villain and evil of all Shakespeare's creations – Iago – the 'demi-devil' whose operations are truly diabolic and cause catastrophe.

The plot of the play *Othello* works on the basis of deception, on the fact that things are not what they seem to be. The entire play dramatises how in both character and in the actions that occur there is a wide discrepancy between what appears to be the case and what in fact constitutes the reality. Iago lies at the pivot of the plot of *Othello*, and his modus operandi gives rise to this form of deception that governs the atmosphere.

Iago is the ensign of Othello, who is the chief General of the Venetian army. Iago is portrayed from the outset as an honest and loyal friend to everyone. In reality, Iago is a devious villain who spends his time spinning a web of lies and deceit that creates havoc for everyone. At the beginning of the play Iago adopts the role of friend and advisor to Roderigo appearing to be loyal and helpful to him and promising him that he will assist him in winning the heart of Desdemona. In reality Iago is using Roderigo simply for his money and jewels: 'Thus do I ever make my fool my purse.'

Othello appears in the opening acts as the very personification of self-control, of the man with so secure a sense of his own worth that nothing can ruffle the calmness of his mind and manner. When Brabantio threatens him with imprisonment, believing he has lured his daughter with witchcraft and magic, Othello calmly shows an exceptional degree of self-control, claiming that he will not run away: 'My parts/my title, and my perfect soul,/ Shall manifest me rightly.' Yet, within days this man who has roamed the wild and savage world unmoved by its terrors, is still capable of believing his wife a whore on the flimsiest of evidence. So our initial impression of Othello is undermined very quickly once the play begins and the insidious effect of Iago's poisoning begins to work. Appearance in this case is acutely different from the underlying reality.

Our initial impression of Desdemona as that of a woman who in her father's words is 'A maiden never bold of spirit/So still and quiet, that her motion/Blush'd at her self'. This impression is shattered when she actually appears before the Venetian senate and boldly and confidently proclaims her love for Othello in no uncertain terms. In her father's eyes Desdemona appeared to be the perfect daughter who is shy, unassuming, obedient and loyal. In reality she is an independent woman who is prepared to follow her husband no matter what the cost: 'Here's my husband/And so much duty as my mother show'd/To you, preferring you before her father,/So much I challenge, that I may profess/Due to the Moor my lord.' So again in the play we witness how appearance can belie the underlying reality – the supposedly innocent, demure Desdemona is a woman who can speak her own mind and knows what she wants when the occasion demands it.

Emilia, Iago's wife, is another woman who is not what she appears to be. Throughout the play, Emilia appears to be a cynical, worldly and vulgar woman who is morally corrupt. She mindlessly hands Desdemona's hanky over to her husband simply to please him, and declares later on that she would have no problem in committing adultery if she could make her husband a monarch. Othello may describe her disparagingly as a 'simple bawd', yet Emilia is a woman who possesses a capacity for heroism and moral courage. While she may appear to be superficial and empty-headed, she shows great courage in defending Desdemona's virtue and verbally attacking the person who concocted slanders against her: 'The Moor's abus'd by some outrageous knave/Some base notorious knave, some scurvy fellow...hell knaw his bones,' she ironically tells her husband in anger.

Emilia is not slow to condemn Othello's action of murdering his wife, telling him he is a 'gull', a 'dolt' and a 'black devil'. This woman who was treated by some of the men in the play as a mere bawd or strumpet ends up sacrificing her life in the service of truth. She dies at the hands of her husband as she defends the honour and virtue of Desdemona, while at the same time exposing the truth about her own husband. 'I'll make thee known/Though I lost twenty lives,' she says as she dies alongside Desdemona. So, in fact, the external representation of Emilia in the play is dramatically different from what constitutes reality.

The theme of appearance and reality play a dramatic part in this tragedy. The leading protagonists in this play are deceived continuously about the actual reality of events. When Michael Cassio allows himself to get drunk on the night when he should have been guarding the citadel, Othello dismisses him on the spot appealing to 'honest Iago' for information about the incident. Othello fails repeatedly to see behind the appearance of Iago to his underlying deviousness of nature and instead confides and trusts in his opinion at all times. This contributes to Othello's downfall and Iago's triumph in this play. It is only in the final scene when appearances have broken down and Iago is seen as what he actually is 'a demi-devil', 'a damned slave', a 'viper', that Othello can penetrate to the truth about what has happened.

All characters mistake appearance for the underlying reality, and they end up misinterpreting the truth about events. The root of this lies in the fact that everyone misconstrues the full nature of Iago believing that he is a good and utterly honest man. Iago manages to spend a great deal of time in the drama spinning a web of lies and falsities about other people which are alien from the reality. In doing this, the leading protagonists (and Othello in particular) act on this mere appearance only to wreak havoc and tragedy in their lives. Part of Othello's tragedy lies in the fact that he takes appearance as the ultimate truth about things and acts on it irrationally. It is only when the damage is done and he has murdered his wife in the concluding scene that the real truth about what has happened is revealed fully to him.

There is no doubt that this theme of appearance and reality is an important one in the context of this tragic play. Given the enormous power of Iago to wield such influence over the main protagonist, Othello, it is understandable how such a situation can cause extreme harm and catastrophe. Tragically, Othello learns too late the dangers of judging on mere appearance. The fatal consequences of taking Iago's ideas at face value and adopting an implicit trust in his words are revealed to Othello all too clearly in the final scene when, in a state of blind passion, he has murdered an innocent woman.

P: 16/18
C: 16/18
L: 15/18
M: 5/6
Total: 52/60

COMMENT

This is quite a good answer on the way in which Appearance and Reality are represented in the play. The writer manages to sustain the response right through each paragraph and to tie up the arguments quite clearly in the conclusion. However, the response is a bit short and repetitive in places. Generally speaking, a Higher Level answer would need two or three more paragraphs.

QUESTIONS

'Othello does not kill Desdemona in jealousy, but from conviction forced on him by the almost superhuman art of Iago.' Discuss this statement with quotation or reference to the play.

ANSWER

It is certainly true that Othello kills his wife on account of the fact that he allows himself to be manipulated into believing she has been unfaithful to him as a result of the sinister wiles and powerful art of Iago. However, Othello makes several comments on his behaviour at the conclusion of the play. He speaks about the fact that he is a man who is not easily aroused to jealousy, but that once jealousy dominates him it causes him to act irrationally: 'Speak of me as I am...Of one not easily jealous, but being wrought/Perplex'd in the extreme.'

For purposes of my answer I would argue, therefore, that Othello is certainly exploited fully by the formidable skill and wiles of Iago, but it is not just Iago who causes the tragedy but Othello himself also freely allows himself to become consumed to an extreme degree by jealousy which ends up confusing his rational faculty and judgement.

Iago's mode of operation in the play is truly sinister and superhuman at every stage in the plot. He manages to make himself impervious and invulnerable to every single character in this play. All characters fall victim to the delusion that he is supremely 'honest' and good. Naturally, Othello's conviction of Iago's integrity and goodness generates a great deal of the power which Iago gains as the plot unfolds. Iago achieves this imperviousness by sowing seeds of doubt in the soul and mind of Othello. In the 'temptation scene' (Act III, scene iii), when Iago's plot is maturing nicely, fate and coincidence play splendidly into the hands of the tempter who uses them supremely well. Cassio has just been interceding with Desdemona for help to gain his position in the army when Iago appears beside Othello who stands alone in a different part of the garden. Iago's sly and subtle insinuations, 'Ha, I like not that', and then his shrewd denial 'No...I cannot think it/That he would sneak away so guilty-like', are effective in planting seeds of doubt in the mindset of the vulnerable Othello. Iago in fact is merely a prompter, a catalyst who uses every opportunity to undermine Othello's faith in his wife.

Iago acts as the archetypal tempter with his deliberately framed statements that are thoroughly ambiguous, and his devious ability to leave many unanswered questions hanging in the air, thus sowing seeds of doubt in Othello. He manages to work on Othello using the subtle tactic of appearing to know more than he does. And of course Othello falls for his devious ploys and skilful art and steadily becomes consumed with anger and jealousy.

Iago's methods are truly phenomenal and superhuman. Having aroused the soul of Othello to an extreme degree of passion, jealousy and anger, Iago proceeds to moralise about the dangers of jealousy. 'Good God, the souls of all my tribe defend/From Jealousy!' he tells Othello in tones of caution, all cleverly designed to precisely inflame the seeds of jealousy within Othello. Othello's quick retort that he, a man of virtue, will never allow himself to be consumed by something as base as jealousy ('Think'st thou I'd make a life of jealousy?') is all cleverly twisted later on by Iago, who uses the Moor's position as outsider to make him feel even more vulnerable.

By the middle of the 'temptation scene' when Iago's poison has worked its way effectively through the soul and mind of Othello we can see the corrosive effect it has caused. In his soliloquy that takes place in the middle of the 'temptation scene', Othello considers the possibilities of living with a wife who is unfaithful. He declares he would rather live like a 'toad' in a 'dungeon' 'Than keep a corner in a thing I love/For other's uses'. The possibility that other people would commit adultery with his wife is horrendous. He actually visualises this situation as a 'forked plague' that appals him. Shortly after this Iago manages to secure Desdemona's hanky, which he decides to plant in Cassio's apartment announcing to himself that such 'trifles light as air/Are to the jealous confirmations strong/As proof of Holy Writ.'

Iago who has an outstanding and superhuman knowledge of human nature has judged Othello perfectly at this stage. Within minutes, Othello's surrender is actually so sudden and complete that it even takes Iago by surprise: 'O grace, O heaven defend me!/Are you a man?' Othello breaks down into an uncontrollable passion and fit of jealousy and actualises this by kneeling and committing himself up to the hands of Iago telling him clearly: 'Within these three days, let me hear thee say/That Cassio's not alive'; 'I will withdraw/To furnish me with some swift means of death/For the fair devil.' Iago has acted as a prompter who has provided the cues while Othello has done the rest. Othello has allowed himself to be deceived and his emotions to be clouded and filled with an inordinate jealousy. It can be seen, therefore, that the combination of Iago's superhuman manner of operating so far in the drama, together with Othello's speedy capitulation to his wiles and inexperience of jealousy and passion have caused this dramatic change in the tragic hero.

After his symbolic kneeling with Iago in an act of unity and dedication to the service of destructive evil, Othello moves forward to complete his pledge of what he sees is justice.

From this point on Othello's actions and speeches betray his inability to live with half knowledge and doubts about his wife's actions. He assumes the worst possible state of circumstances and, dominated by a jealousy which he cannot control or manage, he proceeds to see his wife as a 'subtle bawd', a 'whore' of Venice, who must be destroyed or otherwise she will 'betray more men'. It is in this mindset that Othello sets out to murder his wife as she lies sleeping on the bed.

The subtle poison of Iago's superhuman art and ploys have effectively corroded Othello's pure faith and love for his wife and led the tragic hero to this truly devastating situation where he destroys the only love of his life because of a combination of the villainy of Iago and his own inexperience of jealousy.

Othello's words about himself at the conclusion of the play are a self-indictment on his failures so far. He sees himself as fit only to be damned 'Whip me ye devils/From the possession of this heavenly light'. Othello believes that redemption is no longer an option for him; instead he deserves eternal punishment in hell fire for his misjudgement and deeds. He asks the company present to remember him exactly as he is and not to exaggerate. He speaks calmly and in a controlled voice about his flaws 'of one not easily jealous, but being wrought perplexed in the extreme'. He is seeking to extenuate himself before others and admit sincerely that he has sinned.

It is, therefore, fitting to judge that while Iago operates at every stage in a superhuman manner and with devious and near diabolic arts, simultaneously Othello freely allows himself to be aroused to a state of uncontrolled jealousy that is deadly. So, while it is true to say that Iago certainly possesses truly superhuman and prodigious talents to cause evil, Othello in turn allows himself to be governed by uncontrollable emotions such as jealousy and anger, all of which contribute to the tragedy.

COMMENT

This answer is based on arguing the fact that while Iago possesses superhuman arts, Othello is governed by jealousy in his action of killing his wife Desdemona. The response discusses the nature of jealousy based on Othello's own assessment of his behaviour here at the play's conclusion. The response is original and interesting and the writer sustains the answer through to the conclusion. The use of some repetition weakens the answer, but otherwise it is an example of a very good response.

P: 17/18
C: 17/18
L: 17/18
M: 6/6
Total: 57/60

QUESTIONS

'The temptation scene (Act III, scene iii) is an important turning point in the play in facilitating Iago's plot and undermining Othello's faith in his wife Desdemona.'
Test the truth of this statement and make reference to or quotation from the play in your answer.

ANSWER

This scene Act III, scene iii is obviously vitally important in relation to the play's dramatic design. We come to it, as an audience, already heavily burdened with our foreknowledge of Iago's plans and particularly of his intention to turn Desdemona's goodness into 'the net that shall enmesh them all'. Thus initially we are uneasy by the opening exchange between herself and Cassio, 'Be merry, Cassio/For thy solicitor shall rather die/Than give thy cause away'. It is not surprising then, when Iago and Othello appear, and Cassio slinks 'guilty like' away, that the subsequent exchange between Desdemona and her husband arouses our anxiety.

Desdemona's wheedling approach to Othello ('shall't be shortly?'; 'Shall't be tonight at supper…'; 'Why then tomorrow night on Tuesday morn…'; 'When shall he come?') obviously upsets him, since he knows that he has acted with absolute professional integrity in dismissing his lieutenant. What Desdemona is doing here is to trying to turn this small incident into a test of Othello's love for her, even into a matrimonial power struggle: 'Why this is not a boon…nay when I have a suit/Wherein I mean to touch your love indeed/It shall be full of poise and difficulty/And fearful to be granted.'

Othello's reply, 'I will deny thee nothing…grant me this/To leave me but a little to myself', indicates his sense of feeling he is being badgered. Clearly he does not want to quarrel with her, but it is equally clear that what he is tacitly pleading for is to be allowed an area of professional freedom, in which he may act as he sees fit.

Desdemona leaves on a note of childish playfulness: 'Shall I deny you?…Be it as your fancies teach you,/Whate'er you be, I am obedient'. Again the dramatic irony in her comment is terrible, for Othello will shortly become just what his horrible fancies teach him in a way she could never have foreseen. Her obedience too will later be used by him as though it were proof of the compliance of the prostitute, which in his mind she has become, to the demands of her client: 'And she's obedient, Sir, very obedient.'

Othello however, has already been slightly jolted by Iago's carefully timed suggestion that Cassio appears to have slunk away 'guilty like/Seeing you coming'. He is disturbed enough for dark possibilities to flit across his mind, as is made clear at the close of the exchange between himself and his wife: 'Excellent wretch! Perdition catch my soul/But I do love thee and when I love thee not/Chaos is come again.' He is here reassuring himself that all is well, yet expressing characteristically in words that betray to us his capacity to be shaken to the core.

His speech is a kind of private musing, but is, of course, overheard by Iago, who will make the most of it. Nowhere up to now has Othello quite so obviously worn his heart on his sleeve in relation to his need to love her, the sense that she has become the rivet that secures his life.

In this scene Othello's surrender is so complete and so sudden that it takes even Iago by surprise. The fact is that Iago is no more than the prompter who provides the cues: Othello does the rest. Iago is a catalyst. By the end of the scene, we see that the hero's inflamed imagination replaces Iago as a prompter. From here on, Othello gives as well as takes all the 'cues' himself.

Why is Othello so inflammable? How can Iago so easily ignite him into such a blaze of uncontrollable passion? For A.C. Bradley, Othello is dragged into jealousy against his will; for F.R. Leavis, Othello falls because he is a vicious egotist.

Iago's technique has not been unlike that of Othello: he observes Othello's disposition and taking a 'pliant hour' finds means to deliver 'by parcels' what Othello proves all too ready to listen to. Iago observes and exploits a readiness in Othello to respond from fear of what Iago implies. As the scene proceeds, Othello becomes more and more apprehensive. His imagination hurtles uncontrollably from what might be – the possible – to the probable and finally to the palpable, when fantasy becomes 'probable' fact. Othello's hidden insecurity is such that he swallows the bait laid for him by Iago more promptly perhaps than even the latter had expected.

The initial steps in Othello's capitulation in this scene are clear enough. Iago simply exploits what he has observed of Othello's insecurity in relation to the area of personal feeling. Then he proceeds smoothly from initially calling his nebulous allegations mere 'guesses' to naming them 'conjectures', and finally, and destructively definitive 'observances'.

Iago's crucial little shifts and slides are rendered in vivid and exact detail which we, the spectators, watch in fascinated helplessness. At first, we notice that Iago claims that love and duty force him to 'withhold' information on what he 'thinks': 'though I am bound to every act of duty,/I am not bound to all that slaves are free to:/Utter my thoughts'. Then he goes on by claiming that love and duty now force him to disclose frankly what his 'fears' are: this movement from 'think' to 'fear' will obviously alarm Othello, as it was meant to do. Iago proceeds to 'clarify' in his characteristically insidious fashion, on the nature of his 'fear': 'I speak not yet of proof./Look to your wife.' Again, the mention of 'proof' will further alarm Othello, suggesting as it does, that 'proof' is to be had. Othello's nature quickly supplies a definition to couple with Iago's allegation: his fatal tendency to dread is such that when he glimpses the possibility projected by Iago's insinuations, his fear conducts him inexorably to most 'preposterous conclusions'.

It is noteworthy that, from the outset, Othello shows himself less devastated by Iago's words than by his manner, even his silences and the very vagueness of his initial hints 'Nay, there's more in this/I prithee speak to me as to thy thinkings...give the worst of thoughts/

The worst of words'; 'Therefore these stops of thine fright me more'. The words 'fear' and 'fright' recur continually throughout this scene, as Othello's capacity for dread continues to grow.

What Othello cannot endure, as Iago realises, is ignorance and uncertainty: the unknown terrifies him, filling him with a sense of infinite fear. It is this spectre that Iago raises when at a crucial point in the scene, he introduces the issue of jealousy: 'O beware, my lord of jealousy! It is the green-ey'd monster, which doth mock/That meat it feeds on.' It is because Iago realises how vulnerable Othello is to such doubts and suspicions that he follows up with the speciously pious exclamation: 'Good God, the souls of all my tribe defend/From jealousy.'

Othello denies such shocking suggestions, but the more he protests, the more shakily based does his confidence seem. 'Think'st thou I'd make a life of jealousy…? No, to be once in doubt/Is once to be resolved…Away at once with love or jealousy!'

Iago, having now observed the depth of the fear underlying Othello's brave words now moves in for the kill, and in flat contradiction of what he had implied earlier, now 'decides' that he is in 'love' and 'duty' bound to disclose the basis of his pretended fears: 'I am glad of this; for now I shall have reason/To show the love and duty that I bear you/With franker spirit…I speak not yet of proof./Look to your wife; observe her well with Cassio.'

He goes on to remind Othello of his own superior 'insider's' knowledge of Venetian sexual mores, tacitly implying the Moor's lack of sophistication in such matters: 'I know our country disposition well:/In Venice they do let God see the pranks/They dare not show their husbands…'. And now there comes the insidious reminder: 'She did deceive her father, marrying you…'. At this point Iago pretends to backtrack: 'but I am much to blame./I humbly do beseech you of your pardon/For too much loving you.'

When Othello is left alone, it is clear at once what his state of mind is. His attitude is conditioned by his conviction of Iago's integrity: 'This fellow's of exceeding honesty' and of his belief in the Ensign's knowledge of human nature: 'And knows all qualities, with a learned spirit/Of human dealing.'

The soliloquy also makes plain both his emotional and racial insecurity. He speaks about his own likely unattractiveness to Desdemona: 'Haply, for I am black…or for I am declined/Into the vale of years'. The soliloquy here proves the truth of Othello's earlier assertion that for him 'to be once in doubt/Is once to be resolved'.

From this point onward, Othello's speeches betray his complete inability to live with half-knowledge or to sustain doubts about his own worthiness to be loved. Desdemona's entrance at this point is deeply disconcerting to Othello. 'If she be false, O, then heaven mocks itself/I'll not believe it.'

The symbolic significance of the episode, as well as its tragically ironic resonances are evident. Desdemona seeks to heal the pain in his head, by binding it with her handkerchief, But his fears and doubts prevent him from responding to her and he rejects the napkin. The greatest irony here is that it is precisely this 'too little' handkerchief that will later be the 'trifle light as air' that will lead to the destruction of both.

The ominous implications of Othello's failure to accept Desdemona's remedy is underscored for us by Emilia's comment following the departure of the couple: 'I am glad I have found this napkin...My wayward husband hath a hundred times/Woo'd me to steal it...'

Iago takes the hanky from his wife with great joy and elation and once he packs her off he will clearly use it to further his plot against Othello. From the 'trifle' of the handkerchief he is assured that he can distil a further poison toxic enough to 'burn like the mines of sulphur'. Clearly, Othello's desperation at this stage stems from his uncertainty and now he veers in a near-frenzy between needing to know 'everything', and asserting that he would rather know nothing: 'What sense had I of her stol'n hours of lust?'

Self-pity, but also savage pain, is evident in the exaggeration of what follows: 'I had been happy if the general camp/Pioneers and all had tasted her sweet body/So I had nothing known.' Then finally comes the extraordinary outburst where Othello says farewell to the happy past of soldier's life: 'Farewell the plumed troops and the big wars…all quality/Pride, pomp and circumstance of glorious war…Othello's occupation's gone.' Othello is voicing not a literal, but an emotional truth: if he no longer possesses Desdemona's love, then he feels personally negated at every level of his life, not least that of his profession which most ratified his manhood, 'Chaos' has indeed for him come again.

The remainder of the scene shows Othello torn between hope and dread and reacting with great and increasing violence to his intolerable situation: 'Villain be sure thou prove my love a whore…give me the ocular proof'; 'Make me to see't'. It is clear that at this point Othello turns upon Iago, perhaps even physically threatening him. Iago will at once realise that he is not simply taken aback, but genuinely frightened. He now realises that he must go that potentially dangerous stage further, by producing something more specific, something that may serve as proof. Thus he gives the account of Cassio's talk in his sleep and later mentions the handkerchief.

Othello is now a prey to ungovernable anger and to the compulsive desire for vengeance: 'O that the slave had forty thousand lives, one is too poor, too weak for my revenge.' And finally, the words we have been dreading to hear are spoken: 'Now do I see 'tis true; look here Iago,/All my fond love thus do I blow to heaven./'Tis gone/Arise black vengeance from thy hollow cell/Yield up, O love, thy crown…To tyrannous hate…'.

What Othello is doing here, as a self-protective device, is trying to sow hatred in his heart in place of love, and to seek to make that hatred satisfyingly purposeful by pursuing a policy of revenge on those who have wronged him. This explains what lies behind the extravagant language of the speeches at the conclusion of this scene and the climactic kneeling with Iago 'in the due reverence of a sacred vow'.

The Christian Moor, chief warrior of Christian Venice against 'the general enemy Ottoman', now dedicates himself on his knees to the supernatural powers of 'black vengeance'. When Iago kneels and parodies Othello's oath, as a symbol of his alliance with his 'wronged' general ('Witness you ever burning lights above…What bloody work so ever'), the effect is that of a grotesque travesty of the marriage service, a point accentuated by Iago's final sinister comment: 'I am your own forever'.

Iago's promise to kill Cassio 'my friend is dead:/'Tis done at your request', together with Othello's 'Damn her, lewd minx!./furnish me with some swift means of death/For the fair devil', carry a deadening sense of finality: she is now to him 'the fair devil'.

On stage, this moment where hero and villain kneel side by side in dedication of their souls to the service of destructive evil is extraordinarily effective in a theatrical sense: we sense that it is a pivot on which the rest of the play may well turn. It is clear that in the concluding part of this scene the hero and the villain of the drama are mysteriously coalescing under pressure of the powers of destructive evil.

This scene therefore is a dramatic turning point insofar as it dramatises the profound changes wrought within the soul of Othello, and the consequences in terms of the plot will have tragic repercussions on all the characters in the drama.

COMMENT

This is an excellent answer. The writer analyses each stage of this scene in terms of the development of Iago's plot and the simultaneous loss of faith in Othello about his wife's fidelity. Each point is supported with appropriate and relevant quotation and reference from the scene. The answer makes clear statements on the cumulative effect of this scene within the entire play's structure.

P: 18/18
C: 18/18
L: 18/18
M: 6/6
Total: 60/60

QUESTIONS

'Cassio may be a proper man but he is also an honest fool whose weakness plays no small part in the death of Desdemona.' Discuss this statement with appropriate quotation or reference to the play.

ANSWER

This statement is true. Cassio is a man of integrity 'a proper man' as Iago acknowledges, but he is also an honest fool whose weakness plays no small part in the tragic death of Desdemona.

Cassio is important in the play for many different reasons. He is used as a necessary piece of dramatic machinery to facilitate Iago's devious plans and to wreak his revenge on Othello. Therefore he is not really important as a character in his own right in the play but simply as a scapegoat or pawn to make it easier for Iago's wicked plot to develop and flourish. Yet at the same time, Shakespeare invests his character with some realistic features both positive and negative that make him credible and that serve to undermine and destroy the main protagonists of this play.

We are first introduced to Michael Cassio in the play in the opening scene through the disparaging comments of Iago: 'A fellow almost damned in a fair wife...'; 'Mere prattle without practise is all his soldiership'. These bitter remarks stem from the fact that Othello has promoted Cassio as lieutenant and ignored Iago.

Cassio is not without his weaknesses and these are fully exploited by Iago in order to undermine Othello's faith in Desdemona.

Like Othello, Cassio is subjected to a process of temptation by Iago, and like Othello, he fails in the test. Iago, that expert in probing the weaknesses of people manages to do the same with Cassio the good-looking and capable lieutenant, just as he does in the case of Othello the general.

Basically, Cassio is what we would call a 'decent' individual, a natural charmer, at ease in the company of both men and women, unwilling to hurt people and anxious to be liked by everyone. He is definitely a 'proper man' who is refined and well mannered. But he is morally weak, and these defects and limitations are readily exploited by Iago to undermine Cassio and destroy his reputation and honour.

On the first night in Cyprus, Cassio's desire to be accepted socially is what gives rise to his downfall. Even though he knows that he has 'poor and unhappy brains for drinking', he still allows himself to get drunk. With a ludicrous ease almost, Cassio becomes drunk, and before he knows what has happened, he finds himself stripped of his lieutenancy: 'I love thee Cassio, but never more be officer of mine,' says Othello in full-blown anger.

In this incident he shows irresponsibility and a failure of soldierly duty, since he puts himself at risk for no good reason, having been left in charge of the watch by Othello on that night. While this may seem to be a very small and rather insignificant incident, it will be used by Iago to undermine Cassio's position and blacken his reputation before Othello.

Furthermore, Cassio is quite gullible. He is unable to see through people and his failure here also contributes to the tragic action that ensues later on in the play. This is evident in his relationship with Iago. He misinterprets this man, fully believing he is 'honest' and repeatedly turns to him for advice not realising that the same Iago hates him and is intent on sullying his name and reputation. Shortly after the drunken brawl on the citadel, Cassio goes to Iago treating him as a confidante and gets advice about how to restore his damaged reputation. His action is impulsive and his failure to judge the situation and motivation of the villain simply precipitates Iago's foul plot. Cassio plays into Iago's hands and in his foolishness decides to take his advice and intercede with Desdemona to help regain his position since she is 'so free, so kind, so apt, so blessed a disposition, that/she holds it a vice in her goodness not to do more than/she is requested'.

Armed with what he sees as good advice, Michael Cassio begins to fall into the destructive net that will 'enmesh' the main characters and eventually bring about the death of Desdemona.

From now on Iago's plot flourishes. Cassio's rash action in hiring some musicians to entertain Othello on the morning after the brawl episode only does more damage. This action irritates Othello and alienates Cassio even more.

Iago the conniving opportunist is able to use many of Cassio's entrances and exits in the play to supreme advantage to plant suspicious doubts in Othello's mind that something is going on between Michael Cassio and Desdemona. Of course, Cassio in his innocence fails to notice that anything is amiss. He keeps on insisting to Desdemona that she could regain his position as lieutenant by speaking to Othello.

The fact that Cassio is a natural 'insider' in Venice both socially and professionally helps his reputation as a 'proper man'. He is obviously a gentleman, well educated, polished and refined in manner, someone socially acceptable to the Venetian establishment. He has aided Othello in relation to the latter's wooing of Desdemona.

Professionally, it is obvious that his prospects are bright: he is a new type of career officer, a strategist and theorist, rather than a footslogging practical soldier such as Iago. Iago's bitter comment emphasises this contrast between them: 'That never set a squadron in the field/Nor the division of a battle knows/More than a spinster… Mere prattle without practice/Is all his soldiership'. Professional jealousy of Cassio, linked with a peculiar hatred of Othello for having preferred the other man to himself in relation to the lieutenancy, together with sexual suspicions of both men, are the catalysts cited by Iago as justifications for the initiation of his intrigue against both men.

It is Cassio's weakness that enables Iago to involve him further as instrument and victim in his plot against Othello. Once again, Cassio proves an easy catspaw, as Iago organises a scenario where both men indulge in laughing mockery at the expense of Bianca, the prostitute who has fallen in love with Cassio, while Othello strategically placed by Iago where he can see, but cannot hear them, imagines that they are talking of Desdemona. And then fortuitously, Bianca arrives on the scene, and confronts Cassio with that 'trifle light as air', the handkerchief, which to Othello's inflamed mind is now the final proof needed that Desdemona has indeed betrayed him.

Cassio is readily duped by Iago. 'I never knew a Florentine more kind and honest,' he claims (almost paralleling Othello's words: 'A man he is of honesty and trust'). He takes Iago at face value, partly because of the fact that he is a 'proper man' a man who possesses an open generous nature free from suspicion and petty mistrust. Yet, tragically, this very nature makes him a gullible dupe in the hands of the false Iago and contributes in no small part to Desdemona's death at the conclusion.

Cassio is the one who survives at the conclusion of this tragic play. Even though his weakness has contributed to the tragic events he still remains a loyal and faithful friend as he pleads with Othello: 'Dear general, I did never give you cause.' Cassio remains at the end an ordinary, unheroic man whose simple and upright way of being has been exploited by the villain of the play to wreak havoc and cause tragedy on the people who were closest to him.

COMMENT

This is an answer on the character of Cassio and his function in the plot of the play Othello.

The writer manages to show the nature of Cassio and the manner in which he contributes to the disasters that occur in the tragedy. The answer is quite good and reasonably long. The writer has some lapses in syntax and the language used tends to be a bit repetitive and long-winded.

P: 17/18
C: 17/18
L: 16/18
M: 5/6
Total: 55/60

Reading/seeing *Othello* is a horrifying as well as an uplifting experience.' Would you agree with this statement? Support your answer with quotation or reference to the play.

ANSWER

Although I agree unequivocally with the first half of this statement that watching or reading the play is a truly horrifying experience, I find myself at odds with the fact that it is a play which is uplifting. Overall, I found the experience of both reading and watching the performance of this play to be both dark and tragic.

Throughout its entirety it is easy to identify many horrifying aspects. The first one that I would like to focus on is the matter of Iago's character. As one of Shakespeare's most heinous villains, he is impossible to forget. Perhaps one of the things that make him so terrible is his sheer lack of motivation. As Coleridge wrote about him, he has a 'motiveless malignity'. This makes both his character and plot diabolic and indeed horrifying to witness. He does attempt to justify in some ways his foul plot claiming dubiously that Othello 'hath leaped into my seat' with Emilia, or hinting that he is more worthy of the post of lieutenant than Cassio who he claims is 'Mere prattle without practice' in his profession as a soldier. However, these flimsy reasons do not as such justify such a monstrous course of behaviour as he engages in.

There are more personal aspects to Iago's behaviour that are unsettling to behold. One such example is his cynical intolerance and attitude to love. He automatically equates it with lust and mere sexual gratification, destroying the purity and perfection of love by using some very vulgar and obscene comments: 'Lechery, by his hand: an index and prologue to the history of lust and foul thoughts'. Certainly Iago's language and mode of operation are indeed horrifying.

Another frightening aspect of this play comes in Act III, scene iii, aptly entitled the 'temptation scene'. It is reminiscent of the scene between Eve and the devil disguised as a snake in the Garden of Eden. This biblical story brought about humankind's exposure to misery, death, suffering and pestilence. Likewise, this scene in the garden of the citadel, is the beginning of the main protagonist's downfall. Here, Othello is comparable to Eve, while Iago is the evil snake who tempts and tricks Othello into believing his wife is unfaithful. Just like the eating of the forbidden fruit, this scene has grave consequences on the action of this tragic play.

Another appalling aspect of this play is its many racial and bigoted comments: 'An old black ram/Is tupping your white ewe'; 'Run from her guardage to the sooty bosom/Of such a thing as thou'. Although Othello is hailed as the 'valiant Moor' and 'noble Moor', his race is still a contentious issue. For all his status and military prowess, it appears that in the eyes of his white comrades he is first and foremost black before anything else. It is clear that sixteenth-century Italian society is one with deeply engrained prejudices. For many people being black is associated with the dark arts and with evil. Othello himself is aware of these views and coupled with the fact that he is an outsider to Venetian society it causes him a deep sense of insecurity. Of course, Iago manages to capitalise on all this and exploit it for his own personal vendetta, as he whispers in to the ears of Othello: 'In Venice they do not let God see the pranks/They dare not show their husbands.' These insights into how human nature can behave are truly horrifying.

It is a struggle to find any semblance of inspiration or uplifting moments in this play. One such example is Desdemona's innocence and purity of nature. On the surface this may seem to be uplifting. However, we must remember that it is these virtuous traits that Iago twists and uses to 'make a net that will enmesh them all'. Her goodness is of such an extreme that it becomes the means to destroy her eventually. Her generous efforts to plead for Cassio's cause are misinterpreted as a lover's anguish and an overwrought emotional state on the part of her husband. Her problems are exacerbated by her naivety. As she fails to comprehend the reason for and the extent of Othello's fury, she alternates between laying the blame on herself and 'something of the state'. In doing so she unwittingly contributes to her own death. It could almost be said that goodness and integrity are synonymous with foolishness and gullibility in the play, a fact which makes a reader or audience horrified and shocked. It seems, therefore, that any moment where a reader or audience could feel inspired or uplifted are certainly very few.

Perhaps one of the most powerful pieces of evidence countering the claims of any uplifting qualities to this play is seen in the way Iago skilfully embodies the whole idea of dissimulation, and manages to be so effective as a result. All characters for the entire operation of this play remain blissfully blind to his real nature, mistakenly interpreting his nature as 'honest' and 'good'. His apparent moral transparency fools them all. They repeatedly trust and confide in him. The eventual revelation of the truth underlying his dispositions comes too late: Emilia, Desdemona and Othello are dead. However, the nefarious Iago lives on. Although he is faced with a future of torturous agony and imprisonment, the conclusion fails to be an uplifting experience.

Arguably the only uplifting aspect of this play lies in the moral and emotional development of Emilia's character. At the outset of this play she is a woman who is ignorant of her husband's true nature, who merely acts on his wishes and does not question his motives. 'I nothing but to please his fancy,' she says as she mindlessly picks up Desdemona's hanky with the intention of giving it to him immediately. She does not seem to have the same level of moral integrity as her mistress. She readily admits that she would commit adultery to further Iago's social and professional position even if she had to 'venture purgatory for it'. But Emilia takes a defiant stance when Desdemona is accused of committing adultery. She vociferously condemns Othello's wrongful slander of the 'virtuous Desdemona', 'hath she forsook so many noble matches/To be called whore?'

Upon discovering that he has murdered his wife, she rallies against a vindictive and distraught Othello challenging both he and her husband with the truth: 'O gull, O dolt.../ I'll make thee known/Though I lost twenty lives'. Her determination to expose the truth becomes more important to her than protecting her own life, and in fact it results in her death at the hands of her husband. In giving her life, Emilia not only vindicates the honour and integrity of Desdemona's reputation but exposes the villainy and evil of her own husband's actions. This scene that dramatises her moral transformation is quite inspiring but sadly the culmination of tragic and dispiriting events are so great that it fails to make much of an impact.

While Emilia's moral transformation cannot be disputed together with the fact that Desdemona's virtue and fidelity to her husband remains unsullied yet the events that accumulate at the conclusion are indeed shocking and truly tragic. The final scene which dramatises the death of so many innocent and vulnerable people can only cause one to feel truly shocked and horrified, and to experience a sense of revulsion that such an outcome can be caused by the actions and intentions of one man.

COMMENT

This is an excellent answer that deserves full marks. The answer sustains itself fully right through and it concludes by tying up all the points made and referring back to the central argument, the fact that the play leaves us with a feeling of horror and revulsion.

P: 18/18
C: 18/18
L: 17/18
M: 6/6
Total: 59/60

PAST LEAVING CERTIFICATE QUESTIONS

Sample Questions 1

1. Othello is essentially a noble character, flawed by insecurity and a nature that is naïve and unsophisticated. Discuss.

2. Images of animals, images of storm and images of Heaven and Hell predominate in *Othello*. Discuss the use of such images and the purpose they serve in the play.

Sample Questions 2

1. Othello is the principal agent of his own downfall. Discuss this view.

2. Discuss the importance of the character of Emilia in the play as a whole.

3. 'I am not what I am.' Iago is really the pivotal character in *Othello* who facilitates the evil and weakness of others rather than being the evil genius himself. Discuss this view.

4. The plot of *Othello* lacks credibility from the point of view of characterisation and construction; Desdemona being the most unbelievable of all. Discuss.

DEPARTMENT OF EDUCATION GUIDELINES ON ANSWERING LEAVING CERTIFICATE QUESTIONS

MARKING SCHEME

Clarity of Purpose (P): 18
Coherence of Delivery (C): 18
Efficiency of Language Use (L): 18
Accuracy of Mechanics (M): 6
Total marks available: 60

> i. 'Othello's foolishness rather than Iago's cleverness leads to the tragedy of Shakespeare's *Othello*.' Discuss this statement supporting your answer with the aid of suitable reference to the text.

Expect candidates to engage with the balance of responsibility for the tragedy, focusing on Othello's foolishness and Iago's cleverness. Candidates are free to agree and/or disagree, but they must engage with both aspects of the statement, though not necessarily with equal emphasis.

'Foolishness' may be interpreted as naivety, innocence, jealousy etc.

Candidates may employ focused narrative to illustrate the points they make.

POSSIBLE POINTS

- Iago's superb insight exploits Othello's tragic weakness.
- Naive Othello trusts 'honest' Iago.
- Iago is an opportunist but Othello is easily duped.
- Iago's clever soliloquies/asides influence our vision of Othello's tragedy.
- Othello's foolishness can be seen in the context of Iago's exploitation of others.
- Fate diminishes Othello but elevates Iago.

> ii 'Shakespeare's play *Othello* demonstrates the weakness of human judgement.'
> Discuss this statement supporting your answer with the aid of suitable reference to
> the text.

Candidates are free to agree and/or disagree with the view expressed in the statement, but should focus on the judgements made by the characters in the play.

Candidates may employ focused narrative to illustrate the points they make.

POSSIBLE POINTS

- Othello trusts 'honest' Iago.
- Roderigo is duped by Iago.
- Cassio seeks advice from the man who plots his downfall.
- Initially Emilia evaluates her husband incorrectly.
- Iago's deceptions depend on his clever judgement.
- Desdemona's judgement is questionable.